graphic knits

20 Designs in Bold, Beautiful Color

ALEXIS WINSLOW

 INTERWEAVE.
interweave.com

EDITOR
Erica Smith

TECHNICAL EDITOR
Kristen TenDyke

PHOTOGRAPHER
Joe Hancock

HAIR + MAKEUP
Jessica Shinyeda

ASSOCIATE ART DIRECTOR
Julia Boyles

COVER + INTERIOR DESIGN
Adrian Newman

PRODUCTION
Kerry Jackson

© 2014 Alexis Winslow

Photographs © 2014 Joe Hancock

All rights reserved.

 Interweave
A division of F+W Media, Inc.
4868 Innovation Drive
Fort Collins, CO 80525
interweave.com

Manufactured in China by RR Donnelley
Shenzhen

Library of Congress
Cataloging-in-Publication Data

Winslow, Alexis

Graphic knits : 20 designs in bold,
beautiful color / Alexis Winslow.

pages cm

Includes index.

ISBN 978-1-62033-126-2 (pbk.)

ISBN 978-1-62033-127-9 (PDF)

1. Knitting--Patterns.
2. Dress accessories. I. Title.

TT825.W565 2014

746.43'2--dc23

2014005782

10 9 8 7 6 5 4 3 2 1

acknowledgments

THANK YOU to my darling mother, Jean Tucker, and my talented friend, designer Melissa Wehrle, for helping me knit samples for this book.

Also, a very special thank you to my wonderful husband Brian, for not complaining (all that much) about my yarn hoarding tendencies and for making dinner almost every night while I wrote this book. Support and encouragement from all my friends and family was essential. I am grateful and lucky to have such kind and generous people helping me along my way.

Also, thank you to the yarn companies that generously provided the beautiful materials for the samples in this book:

Austermann Skacel	Louet
Berroco	Madelinetosh
Blue Sky Alpacas	Mulabrigo
Cascade Yarns	Quince & Co.
The Fibre Company	Rowan

CONTENTS

introduction

DOORS OPEN, DOORS CLOSE: WEST 4TH STREET, 14TH STREET, 23RD, AND SO FORTH. I ride the subway every day, my knitting bag in tow. With each passing station, interesting characters wearing interesting garments come and go, and all the while I make steady progress toward my destination and on my project.

Knitting makes me treasure these otherwise tedious moments because it's transformative: making yarn into sweaters, making ordinary girl into creator of extraordinary things—all during my daily commute.

I'm fascinated by this idea of transformation. As a designer and an artist, I think a lot about the potential of raw materials and the potential of the people who knit my patterns. With each new project there is opportunity to grow as a craftsperson, to incorporate new skills. And each new skill has the power to transform you just a little more, expanding your creative potential.

Writing *Graphic Knits* was a project on a grand scale. The garments in this book feature an interplay of color, shapes, and texture that I found fun to create, and often yielded surprising results. The experience pushed me to grow as a designer, to refine my aesthetic, to think about every detail. I tried to not only write thoughtful patterns, but also create an entertaining knitting experience. This special bit of knitting magic is something that is understood by every knitter who has ever followed a pattern. It's that unexplainable craving for just one more row.

As you work through the pages of my book, I hope you look for opportunities to transform yourself into a master of your craft. I hope the patterns not only produce beautiful garments, but also help you become a better, more curious knitter. And above all else, I hope you have fun.

Alexis Winslow

minnow top

THIS LOOSE, LACY TOP SHOWS how the concept of "graphic" can be interpreted through texture as well as color. The openwork chevron patterning makes this a beautiful layering piece for any time of year. The top is meant to be worn with a lot of positive ease for an unfussy look. An i-cord tie a few inches below the waist gives this top an elegant, feminine touch and accentuates the beautiful drape and sheen of the light, lacy fabric. The neck is edged with a simple rolled hem for a soft, easy finish. The lace is surprisingly fun and easy to knit, and will keep you always wanting to knit just a little more

FINISHED SIZE

32½ (36½, 41, 45)" (82.5 [92.5, 104, 114.5] cm) bust circumference.

Garment shown measures 32¼" (82.5 cm)

YARN

Sport weight (#2 Fine)

Shown here: Blue Sky Alpacas Metalico (50% baby alpaca, 50% mulberry silk; 147 yd [135 m]/50 g): #1615 Cinnabar, 5 (5, 6, 6) skeins.

NEEDLES

Body: Size U.S. 8 (5 mm): straight.

Neck Edging: Size U.S. 8 (5 mm): 16" (40 cm) circular (cir).

I-cord Tie: Size U.S. 8 (5 mm): set of 2 double-pointed (dpn).

Adjust needle size if necessary to obtain the correct gauge.

NOTIONS

Stitch markers (m)

8 removable stitch markers (safety pins are great)

Stitch holders or waste yarn

Yarn needle

GAUGE

19 sts and 26 rows = 4" (10 cm) in Chart A.

Front

With straight needles, CO 77 (87, 97, 107) sts.

Knit 5 rows.

SET-UP ROW (WS): K3, place m (pm), purl to last 3 sts, pm, k3.

EST PATT (RS): Work 3 sts in Gtr st (knit all sts, every row), sl m, work to next m in Chart A, sl m, work last 3 sts in Gtr St.

Cont to work Chart A until Rows 1–36 have been completed 4 times. (Piece should meas about 23" [58.5 cm] to here.)

Left Shoulder

DIVIDE FOR NECK (RS): K28 (31, 35, 39), k2tog, k1, put the next 15 (19, 21, 23) sts on a holder for neck front, and keeping the marker intact put the last 31 (34, 38, 42) sts on a separate holder for right shoulder—30 (33, 37, 41) sts rem for left shoulder.

NEXT ROW (WS): Purl to m, sl m, k3.

NEXT ROW (RS): Knit to last 3 sts, k2tog, k1—29 (32, 36, 40) sts rem.

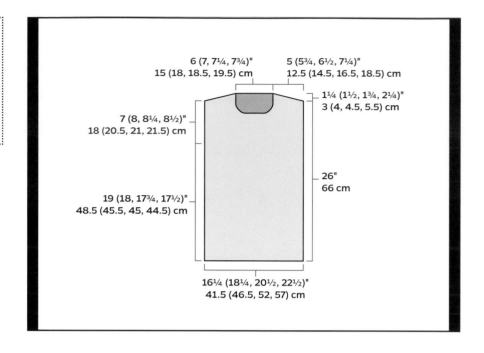

6 (7, 7¼, 7¾)"
15 (18, 18.5, 19.5) cm

5 (5¾, 6½, 7¼)"
12.5 (14.5, 16.5, 18.5) cm

1¼ (1½, 1¾, 2¼)"
3 (4, 4.5, 5.5) cm

7 (8, 8¼, 8½)"
18 (20.5, 21, 21.5) cm

26"
66 cm

19 (18, 17¾, 17½)"
48.5 (45.5, 45, 44.5) cm

16¼ (18¼, 20½, 22½)"
41.5 (46.5, 52, 57) cm

Shape Shoulder with Short-Rows (see Techniques)

SHORT-ROW 1: Purl to 2 sts before m, w&t, knit to last 3 sts, k2tog, k1—28 (31, 35, 39) sts rem.

SHORT-ROW 2: Purl to 4 sts before m, w&t, knit to last 3 sts, k2tog, k1—27 (30, 34, 38) sts rem.

SHORT-ROW 3: Purl to 6 sts before m, w&t, knit to last 3 sts, k2tog, k1—26 (29, 33, 37) sts rem.

SHORT-ROW 4: Purl to 8 sts before m, w&t, knit to last 3 sts, k2tog, k1—25 (28, 32, 36) sts rem.

Sizes 36½ (41, 45)" only:

SHORT-ROW 5: Purl to 10 sts before m, w&t, knit to last 3 sts, k2tog, k1—27 (31, 35) sts rem.

Sizes 41 (45)" only:

SHORT-ROW 6: Purl to 12 sts before m, w&t, knit to end.

Size 45" only:

SHORT-ROW 7: Purl to 14 sts before m, w&t, knit to end.

All Sizes:

Short-row shaping is complete. Incorporate the wraps on the next row as you pass them.

Size 32½" only:

NEXT ROW (WS): Purl to m, sl m, k3.

DEC ROW (RS): Knit to last 3 sts, k2tog, k1—24 sts rem.

Sizes 36½ (41, 45)" only:

NEXT ROW (WS): Purl to m, sl m, k3.

NEXT ROW (RS): Knit.

Rep the last 2 rows 0 (0, 1) times.

All sizes:

Knit 2 rows.

NEXT ROW (WS): Purl to m, sl m, k3.

EST PATT (RS): Work 3 sts in Gtr St, sl m, work 21 (21, 26, 31) sts in Chart

CHART A

Row numbers (right side): 35, 33, 31, 29, 27, 25, 23, 21, 19, 17, 15, 13, 11, 9, 7, 5, 3, 1

CHART B

Row numbers (right side): 31, 29, 27, 25, 23, 21, 19, 17, 15, 13, 11, 9, 7, 5, 3, 1

Legend

☐	Knit on RS, purl on WS	○	yo
•	Purl on RS, knit on WS	⋀	s2kp
╱	k2tog	▢	pattern repeat
╲	ssk		

A (A, B, A), work 0 (3, 2, 1) sts in St st (knit on RS, purl on WS).

Work Rows 2–13 of chart as est.

Break yarn and put the 24 (27, 31, 35) left shoulder sts on a holder, keeping the m in place.

Right Shoulder

Place the 31 (34, 38, 42) held right front sts onto your needle and join yarn to beg working a RS row.

DEC ROW (RS): K1, ssk, knit to end—1 st dec'd.

NEXT ROW (WS): K3, sl m, purl to end.

Rep the last 2 rows once—29 (32, 36, 40) sts rem.

Shape Shoulder with Short-Rows

SHORT-ROW 1: K1, ssk, knit to 2 sts before m, w&t, purl to end—28 (31, 35, 39) sts rem.

SHORT-ROW 2: K1, ssk, knit to 4 sts before m, w&t, purl to end—27 (30, 34, 38) sts rem.

SHORT-ROW 3: K1, ssk, knit to 6 sts before m, w&t, purl to end—26 (29, 33, 37) sts rem.

SHORT-ROW 4: K1, ssk, knit to 8 sts before m, w&t, purl to end—25 (28, 32, 36) sts rem.

Sizes 36½ (41, 45)" only:

SHORT-ROW 5: K1, ssk, knit to 10 sts before m, w&t, purl to end—27 (31, 35) sts rem.

Sizes 41 (45)" only:

SHORT-ROW 6: Knit to 12 sts before m, w&t, purl to end.

Size 45" only:

SHORT-ROW 7: Knit to 14 sts before m, w&t, purl to end.

All Sizes:

Short-row shaping is complete. Incorporate the wraps on the next row as you pass them.

Size 32½" only:

DEC ROW (RS): K1, ssk, knit to end—24 sts rem.

Knit 2 rows.

Size 45" only:

NEXT ROW (RS): Knit.

NEXT ROW (WS): K3, sl m, purl to end.

Sizes 36½ (41, 45)" only:

Knit 3 rows.

All Sizes:

NEXT ROW (WS): K3, sl m, purl to end.

EST PATT (RS): Work 0 (3, 2, 1) sts in St st, work Row 1 (1, 19, 1) of Chart A (A, B, A) to m, sl m, work last 3 sts in Gtr St.

Work Rows 2 (2, 20, 2)–13 (13, 31, 13) of chart as est.

Keep sts on needle and yarn attached.

Back

Join the right and left shoulder pieces together as follows:

JOINING ROW (WS): K3, purl to end of right shoulder sts, use the backward loop method (see Techniques) to CO 29 (33, 35, 37) sts, place the 24 (27, 31, 35) held left shoulder sts onto empty needle and purl to m, sl m, k3—77 (87, 97, 107) sts.

Work Rows 15–29 of Chart A between the markers while maintaining the 3 Gtr Sts outside of the markers.

Back Shoulders
Shape Shoulders with Short-Rows

> ***Note:*** *When working wrapped stitches from a previous short-row, always incorporate the wraps.*

SHORT-ROW 1: K3, sl m, purl to 8 (10, 12, 14) sts before m, w&t; knit to 8 (10, 12, 14) sts before m, w&t;

SHORT-ROW 2: Purl to 6 (8, 10, 12) sts before m, w&t; knit to 6 (8, 10, 12) sts before m, w&t;

SHORT-ROW 3: Purl to 4 (6, 8, 10) sts before m, w&t; knit to 4 (6, 8, 10) sts before m, w&t;

SHORT-ROW 4: Purl to 2 (4, 6, 8) sts before m, w&t; knit to 2 (4, 6, 8) sts before m, w&t;

Tie It Up

The tie is optional, and in fact this top looks great when worn without it. But since we are creative creatures, why not have some fun? As an alternative to the i-cord tie, you can use a double-sided satin ribbon, or a twisted metallic cord, or a rustic-looking twill tape finished with several large wooden beads at the ends. Working the i-cord in a contrasting color of the same yarn is another creative idea. If you choose to use a contrasting color of yarn, a nice touch is to use that same yarn to work the garter stitch edging at the bottom and the neck edging.

Sizes 36½ (41, 45)" only:

SHORT-ROW 5: Purl to 2 (4, 6) sts before m, w&t; knit to 2 (4, 6) sts before m, w&t;

Sizes 41 (45)" only:

SHORT-ROW 6: Purl to 2 (4) sts before m, w&t; knit to 2 (4) sts before m, w&t;

Size 45" only:

SHORT-ROW 7: Purl to 2 sts before m, w&t; knit to 2 sts before m, w&t;

All Sizes:

Short-row shaping is complete.

NEXT ROW (WS): K3, purl to m, sl m, k3.

NEXT ROW (RS): Knit.

NEXT ROW (WS): K3, purl to m, sl m, k3.

Rep the last 2 rows once more.

Knit 3 rows.

Work Rows 30–36 from Chart A, maintaining the 3 Gtr Sts outside the markers

Work Rows 1–36 from Chart A 3 times.

Work Rows 1–26 from Chart A.

Knit 5 rows, ending after a RS row.

BO very loosely kwise.

Finishing

Block to measurements with the garment folded in half at the shoulder. Let it dry completely before moving.

SEW SIDE SEAMS: Place a removable m on each edge of front and back 2½" (6.5 cm) from the lower edges. Place another removable m on each edge of front and back 7 (8, 8¼, 8½)" (18 [20.5, 21, 21.5] cm) from the top of the folded edge (for the armholes). Thread a yarn needle with the same yarn, and use the mattress stitch to sew the side seams on each edge between the markers. Remove markers.

Neck Edging

With the RS facing, and cir needles, beg at the top of the left shoulder, pick up and knit 9 (10, 12, 14) sts along the vertical edge of the neck, 11 sts along the diagonal edge, place the 15 (19, 21, 23) held front neck sts onto empty needle and knit across, pick up and knit 11 sts along the other diagonal edge, 9 (10, 12, 14) sts along the other vertical edge, then 29 (33, 35, 37) sts along the back of the neck—84 (94, 102, 110) sts. Pm for beg of rnd.

Knit 5 rnds. BO loosely. Tug the BO edge width-wise to encourage the St st fabric to roll.

I-Cord Tie

With dpn, CO 3 sts. Work an i-cord (see Techniques) over these 3 sts until the cord meas about 63 (68, 73, 78)" (160 [172.5, 185.5, 198] cm).

Using a yarn needle with a large eye, thread the i-cord through the second row of eyelets beg about 6" (15 cm) from the right edge and working in and out through the eyelets all the way around.

Weave in loose ends.

rockling
cardigan

THIS COZY TOP-DOWN cardigan uses an easy slip-stitch technique to create woven-looking textured stripes. The design features a large shawl collar, shaped to lie naturally with no fuss. Pockets are optional and are worked into the body of the sweater. The sweater closes with five large buttons starting just below the bust.

FINISHED SIZE
About 30 (33, 37, 40, 44)" (76 [84, 94, 101.5, 112] cm) bust circumference, buttoned with 2½" (6.5 cm) overlapping button band.

Cardigan shown measures 33" (84 cm).

YARN
Worsted weight (#4 Medium)

Shown here: Cascade Yarns Eco + (100% Highland Peruvian Wool; 478 yd [437 m]/250 g): #507 Lipstick (A), 2 (2, 2, 3, 3) skeins; #9002 Tarnish Platinum Twist (B), 1 skein.

NEEDLES
Size U.S. 10 (6 mm): 24" (61 cm) circular (cir) and set of double-pointed (dpn).

Adjust needle size if necessary to obtain the correct gauge.

NOTIONS
Stitch markers (m)

2 removable markers (safety pins are fine)

Stitch holders or waste yarn

Yarn needle

Five 1" (2.5 cm) buttons

Sewing needle and matching thread (color A) for buttons

5 backing ⅝" (1.5 cm) buttons (optional; see sidebar)

GAUGE
16 sts and 23½ rows = 4" (10 cm) in stockinette stitch.

Stitch Guide

Slip Stitch Pattern
(also see chart)

Flat (multiple of 2 sts)

ROW 1 (RS): Change to color B, k1, *sl 1 pwise wyf, k1; rep from * to last st, k1.

ROW 2: Purl.

ROW 3: Change to color A, k2, *sl 1 pwise wyf, k1; rep from *.

ROW 4: Purl.

Work Rows 1–4 for patt.

Circular (multiple of 2 sts)

RND 1: Change to color B, k1, *sl 1 pwise wyf, k1; rep from * to last st, k1.

RND 2: Knit.

RND 3: Change to color A, k2, *sl 1 pwise wyf, k1; rep from *.

RND 4: Knit.

Work Rnds 1–4 for patt.

Notes

During raglan shaping, there is one more stitch on right front than on left front because extra stitch on right front is used between increases on raglan shaping. That extra stitch on left of sweater falls on sleeve.

When working stripes, carry unused color along side by twisting two colors together at beginning of row or rnd.

Yoke

With color A and cir needles, CO 36 (38, 44, 46, 52) sts.

SET-UP ROW (WS): P2 for right front, pm, p7 (7, 9, 9, 11) for right sleeve, pm, p19 (21, 23, 25, 27) for back, pm, p7 (7, 9, 9, 11) for left sleeve, pm, p1 for left front.

Shape Raglan

RAGLAN INC ROW (RS): *Knit to m, M1, sl m, k1, M1; rep from * 3 more times, knit to end—8 sts inc'd.

Purl 1 WS row.

Rep last 2 rows 11 times—132 (134, 140, 142, 148) sts; 14 sts on right front, 13 sts on left front, 31 (31, 33, 33, 35) sts each sleeve, and 43 (45, 47, 49, 51) sts for back.

Work Rows 1–4 of Slip St Patt. Break yarn for color B.

[Work Raglan Inc Row, then purl 1 WS row] 6 (8, 4, 4, 0) times—180 (198, 172, 174, 148) sts; 20 (22, 18, 18, 14) sts on right front, 19 (21, 17, 17, 13) sts on left front, 43 (47, 41, 41, 35) sts each sleeve, and 55 (61, 55, 57, 51) sts for back.

Shape Neck and Raglan

Sizes 37 (40, 44)" only:

NECK AND RAGLAN INC ROW (RS): K2, M1, *knit to m, M1, sl m, k1, M1; rep from * 3 more times, knit to last 2 sts, M1, k2—10 sts inc'd.

Purl 1 WS row.

[Work Raglan Inc Row, then purl 1 WS row] 3 times.

Rep the last 8 rows 0 (0, 2) times—206 (208, 250) sts; 23 (23, 29) sts on right front, 22 (22, 28) sts on left front, 49 (49, 59) sts each sleeve, and 63 (65, 75) sts for back.

Sizes 37 (40)" only:

NECK AND RAGLAN INC ROW (RS): K2, M1, *knit to m, M1, sl m, k1, M1; rep from * 3 more times, knit to last 2 sts, M1, k2—10 sts inc'd.

Purl 1 WS row.

[Work Raglan Inc Row, then purl 1 WS row] 1 (2) times—224 (234) sts; 26 (27) sts on right front, 25 (26) sts on left front, 53 (55) sts each sleeve, and 67 (71) sts for back.

Sizes 30 (37, 40)" only:

Work 4 (2, 2) rows even in St st (knit on RS, purl on WS), ending after a WS row.

SLIP STITCH CHART

☉	with color A knit on RS, purl on WS
‖	with color B knit on RS, purl on WS
⌄	sl st pwise wyf
☐	pattern repeat

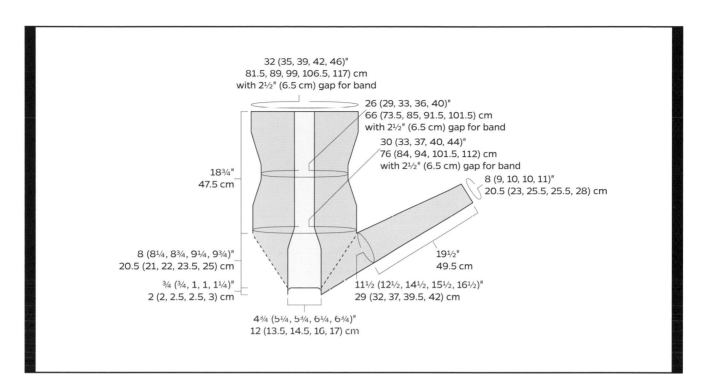

32 (35, 39, 42, 46)"
81.5, 89, 99, 106.5, 117) cm
with 2½" (6.5 cm) gap for band

26 (29, 33, 36, 40)"
66 (73.5, 85, 91.5, 101.5) cm
with 2½" (6.5 cm) gap for band

30 (33, 37, 40, 44)"
76 (84, 94, 101.5, 112) cm
with 2½" (6.5 cm) gap for band

8 (9, 10, 10, 11)"
20.5 (23, 25.5, 25.5, 28) cm

18¾"
47.5 cm

8 (8¼, 8¾, 9¼, 9¾)"
20.5 (21, 22, 23.5, 25) cm

¾ (¾, 1, 1, 1¼)"
2 (2, 2.5, 2.5, 3) cm

19½"
49.5 cm

11½ (12½, 14½, 15½, 16½)"
29 (32, 37, 39.5, 42) cm

4¾ (5¼, 5¾, 6¼, 6¾)"
12 (13.5, 14.5, 16, 17) cm

Sizes 30 (33, 40, 44)" only:

NECK INC ROW (RS): K2, M1, knit to last 2 sts, M1, k2—182 (200, 236, 252) sts; 21 (23, 28, 30) sts on right front, 20 (22, 27, 29) sts on left front, 43 (47, 55, 59) sts each sleeve, and 55 (61, 71, 75) sts on back.

Purl 1 WS row.

Sizes 33 (44)" only:

Work 2 rows even in St st, ending after a WS row.

Divide Body And Sleeves

All Sizes:

NEXT ROW (RS): K20 (22, 25, 27, 29) to first m, remove m, k1 (1, 1, 1, 2), put next 42 (46, 52, 54, 56) sts on a holder, use the backward loop method (see Techniques) to CO 4 (4, 6, 8, 10) sts, k0 (0, 0, 0, 1), remove m, k55 (61, 67, 71, 75) to next m, remove m, k1 (1, 1, 1, 2), put next 42 (46, 52,

54, 56) sts on a holder, CO 4 (4, 6, 8, 10) sts, k0 (0, 0, 0, 1), remove m, k21 (23, 26, 28, 30) to end—106 (116, 132, 144, 160) sts rem for body.

Body

Work 5 (3, 1, 5, 3) rows even in St st, ending after a WS row.

Shape Neck

NECK INC ROW (RS): K2, M1, knit to last 2 sts, M1, k2—2 sts inc'd.

Work 7 rows even in St st.

Rep the last 8 rows once more— 110 (120, 136, 148, 164) sts.

Sizes 33 (37, 40, 44)" only:

Rep Neck Inc Row—122 (138, 150, 166) sts.

All Sizes:

Place a removable marker in first and last st of row. These markers will be used later for knitting button band.

Work 3 (4, 6, 0, 0) rows even in St st, ending after a RS row.

Shape Waist

PLACE MARKERS FOR WAIST SHAPING (WS): P9 (10, 12, 14, 16), pm, p32 (36, 40, 42, 46), pm, p28 (30, 34, 38, 42), pm, p32 (36, 40, 42, 46), pm, p9 (10, 12, 14, 16).

Work Rows 1–4 of Slip St Patt.

WAIST DEC ROW (RS): *Knit to m, sl m, ssk, knit to 2 sts before next m, k2tog, sl m; rep from * once more, knit to end—4 sts dec'd; 106 (118, 134, 146, 162) sts rem.

Purl 1 WS row.

Work Row 1 of Slip St Patt.

Cont with color B as foll:

Work 3 rows even in St st with color B.

Rep Waist Dec Row—102 (114, 130, 142, 158) sts rem.

Work 3 rows even in St st, ending after a WS row.

Work Rows 3 and 4 of Slip St Patt.

Cont with color A as foll:

Rep Waist Dec Row—98 (110, 126, 138, 154) sts rem.

Purl 1 WS row.

Work Rows 1–4 of Slip St Patt.

Cont with color A as foll:

Rep Waist Dec Row—94 (106, 122, 134, 150) sts rem.

Purl 1 WS row.

Work Row 1 of Slip St Patt.

Cont with color B as foll:

Work 7 rows even in St st, ending after a WS row.

Work Rows 3 and 4 of Slip St Patt.

Cont with color A as foll:

WAIST INC ROW (WS): *Knit to m, sl m, M1, knit to next m, M1, sl m; rep from * once more, knit to end—98 (110, 126, 138, 154) sts.

Purl 1 WS row.

Work Rows 1–4 of Slip St Patt.

Cont with color A as foll:

Rep Waist Inc Row—102 (114, 130, 142, 158) sts; 9 (10, 12, 14, 16) sts each front, 28 (32, 36, 38, 42) sts each side and 28 (30, 34, 38, 42) sts for back.

(Body should meas about 11 [11, 11, 10¾, 10½]" (29 [28, 28, 27.5, 26.5] cm) from underarm.)

If you don't want pockets:

Work 5 rows even in St st, ending after a WS row.

Rep last 6 rows once more—106 (118, 134, 146, 162) sts.

If you do want pockets:

POCKET SET-UP ROW (WS): P4 (5, 6, 7, 8), pm, put next 20 (20, 22, 24, 24) sts on a st holder or waste yarn removing m, use the backward loop method to CO 20 (20, 22, 24, 24) sts, pm, purl to 15 (15, 16, 17, 16) sts before last m, pm, put next 20 (20, 22, 24, 24) sts on a st holder or waste yarn removing m, CO 20 (20, 22, 24, 24) sts, pm, purl to end.

EST POCKET RIBBING (RS): Knit to m, [p1, k1] to next m, sl m, knit to second to last m, [p1, k1] to next m, knit to end.

Work 3 rows even as est, ending after a WS row.

BODY SET-UP AND WAIST INC ROW (RS): K9 (10, 12, 14, 16) removing first pocket m as you pass it, pm, M1, knit to next pocket m, remove m, knit to next m, M1, sl m, knit to next m, sl m, M1, knit to next pocket m, remove m, k15 (15, 16, 17, 16), M1, pm, knit to end removing last pocket m as you pass it—106 (118, 134, 146, 162) sts.

Work 5 rows even in St st, ending after a WS row.

Both Pocket Options Resume Instructions:

Rep Waist Inc Row—110 (122, 138, 150, 166) sts.

Work 3 rows even in St st, ending after a WS row.

Work Rows 1 and 2 of Slip St Patt.

Cont with color B as foll:

Rep Waist Inc Row—114 (126, 142, 154, 170) sts.

Purl 1 WS row.

Work Rows 3 and 4 of Slip St Patt, then work Rows 1 and 2.

Cont with color B as foll:

Rep Waist Inc Row—118 (130, 146, 158, 174) sts.

Purl 1 WS row.

Break yarn for color B.

Work Rows 3 and 4 of Slip St Patt.

Cont with color A as foll:

Work even in St st until piece meas 15¾" (40 cm) from divide, ending after a WS row.

EST RIBBING (RS): K2, *p2, k2; rep from *.

NEXT ROW (WS): P2, *k2, p2; rep from *.

Rep the last 2 rows for 3" (7.5 cm).

BO very loosely in rib.

Sleeve

Slip 42 (46, 52, 54, 56) held sts from one sleeve onto 3 dpn. With color A and an empty dpn, beg at center of underarm, pick up and knit 2 (2, 3, 4, 5) sts from cast-on edge, knit to end of held sts, pick up and knit another 2 (2, 3, 4, 5) sts. Pm for beg of rnd and join ends to work in rnd—46 (50, 58, 62, 66) sts.

Size 37" only:

DEC RND: Ssk, knit to last 2 sts, k2tog—56 sts rem.

All Sizes:

Knit 11 (13, 8, 23, 23) rnds.

Shape Sleeve

> **Note:** Read the following instructions carefully before cont; Slip St Patt is worked at the same time as the sleeve shaping.)

DEC RND: Ssk, knit to 2 sts before end, k2tog—2 sts dec'd.

Knit 11 (11, 11, 5, 5) rnds.

Rep the last 12 (12, 12, 6, 6) rnds 6 (6, 7, 10, 10) times—32 (36, 40, 40, 44) sts rem; and at the same time cont working Slip St Patt as follows:

Knit 13 (13, 19, 7, 7) rnds with color A.

*Work Rnds 1–4 of Slip St Patt.

Knit 2 rnds with color A.

Work Rnd 1 of Slip St Patt.

Knit 7 rnds with color B.

Work Rnd 3 of Slip St Patt.

Knit 3 rnds with color A.

Rep from * once more.

Work Rnds 1–4 of Slip St Patt.

Knit 16 rnds with color A.

Work Rnd 1 of Slip St Patt.

Knit 3 rnds with color B.

Work Rnds 3 and 4 of Slip St Patt, then work Rnds 1 and 2.

Knit 2 rnds with B.

Work Rnd 3 of Slip St Patt.

Break yarn for color B and cont with color A only.

Knit until piece meas 16½" (42 cm) from divide.

Cuff

Est Ribbing: *K2, p2; rep from *.

Cont to work as est for 3" (7.5 cm).

BO very loosely in rib.

Make second sleeve the same as the first.

Finishing

Block piece to measurements.

Collar and Band

The collar and button band are worked together at same time from stitches picked up from around the front opening. Short-rows create a cozy shawl collar, and strategically placed increases ensure that the collar will always lie flat. For best results when picking up stitches on selvedge edge, try to follow a single column of stitches all the way up, and work about 1 stitch away from edge.

With cir needle and color A, beg at lower edge of right front, pick up and knit 11 sts along side of ribbing section, 40 (45, 45, 50, 50) sts to removable m, pm, pick up and knit 44 (42, 42, 40, 42) sts up to CO edge, pm, pick up and knit 36 (38, 44, 46, 52) along CO edge (1 st in each st), pm, pick up and knit 44 (42, 42, 40, 42) sts along neck edge to second removable m, pm, pick up and knit 40 (45, 45, 50, 50) sts to ribbing section, 11 sts to edge—226 (234, 240, 248, 258) sts.

EST RIBBING (WS): P2 (2, 0, 0, 2), *k2, p2; rep from *.

The rest of collar and band section is worked in 2 × 2 rib as est on last row. As you inc sts to shape collar, maintain 2 × 2 ribbing pattern in each section between markers.

Begin Short-Row Shaping (see Techniques)

SHORT-ROW 1 (RS): Work to last m, sl m, w&t; sl m, work to last m, sl m, w&t;

SHORT-ROW 2: Work to 4 sts before last m, w&t; work to 4 sts before last m, w&t;

SHORT-ROW 3: Work to 4 sts before wrapped st of previous row, w&t; work to 4 sts before wrapped st of previous row, w&t;

Rep the last short-row 2 more times.

NEXT 2 ROWS: Work to end of row, incorporating all wraps as you pass them.

INC ROW (RS): *Work to first m, sl m, M1, work to next m, M1, sl m; rep from * once more, work to end of row—4 sts inc'd.

Work 1 WS row even.

Rep the last 2 rows once more—234 (242, 248, 256, 266) sts.

BUTTONHOLE AND INC ROW (RS): Work 7 (5, 5, 7, 5) sts, ssk, [yo] twice, k2tog, *work 7 (7, 7, 6, 7) sts, ssk, [yo] twice, k2tog; rep from * 3 more times, sl m, M1, work to next m, M1, sl m, work to next m, sl m, M1, work to next m, M1, sl m, work to end of row—238 (246, 252, 260, 270) sts.

Work 1 WS row even working double yarn-overs as follows: knit into first yarn-over normally, then knit through the back loop of the second yarn-over.

Rep Inc Row—242 (250, 256, 264, 270) sts.

Work 3 rows even, ending after a WS row.

Using a Backing Button

There are many ways to sew buttons to hand knits, but for garments like this one I prefer to use a backing button. Using a large heavy button alone can cause fabric to distort and button to dangle or sag. Sewing an extra button to the back will keep your stitches looking nice and neat for years to come.

Backing buttons should be very lightweight and about half the diameter of the front button. I usually buy thin clear plastic buttons or buttons that match the color of fabric. For garments that are mostly worn open and where the inside might show as much as the outside, it's also a nice touch to use the same buttons for front and back. This is only preferable if the buttons are small and lightweight.

Here's how I do it:

STEP 1: Thread a sewing needle with a coordinating thread, leaving a long uneven tail.

STEP 2: Pull thread in and out of backing button, pulling button to end of thread tail. Tie the 2 ends of thread together with a simple square knot, and pull knot so that it is right up against button.

STEP 3: Pull needle through knitted fabric, then through regular button, and back through fabric and backing button. Repeat this step several times to sew button to garment, being sure to keep a little slack in the thread between the buttons.

STEP 4: Pull needle to front side, but not through holes in button. Wrap thread around the threads between the knitted fabric and the regular button several times to create a shank.

STEP 5: Poke tip of needle through middle of shank, wrap thread around tip of needle 3 times to create a knot. Pull needle through, tightening knot as you go.

STEP 6: Secure end by pulling needle through shank several more times. Snip thread close to base.

Begin Short-Row Shaping:

> **Note:** Incorporate all wraps as you pass them.

SHORT-ROW 1 (RS): Work to 16 sts before last m, w&t; work to 16 sts before last m, w&t;

SHORT-ROW 2: Work to wrapped st from previous row, work 4 sts, w&t; work to wrapped st from previous row, work 4 sts, w&t;

Rep the last short-row 3 more times.

NEXT ROW (RS): Work to end of row.

BO very loosely in rib, using a larger needle held in your right hand if necessary.

Pocket Lining

Transfer held pocket sts onto needle preparing to work a RS row.

With empty needle and color A, use the backward loop method to CO 1 st, knit across 20 (20, 22, 24, 24) held sts, CO 1 st—22 (22, 24, 26, 26) sts.

Work even in St st until pocket reaches ¼" (6 mm) short of lower edge of cardigan, or to your desired depth.

BO all sts.

Make second pocket lining the same as the first.

Using a yarn needle threaded with color A, sew pocket lining to inside of cardigan. Be careful that your sts are invisible from the RS.

Arrange cardigan on a table overlapping front bands with buttonhole side on top. Use buttonholes to help you mark placement of each button on other side of band, being careful to space buttons evenly. Using a sewing needle and thread, sew 5 buttons to front of cardigan. Use a clear or matching color button on back side wto prevent sts around button from pulling or distorting (see sidebar).

Weave in loose ends. Lightly block the collar and pockets so they lie flat.

rook pullover

THIS TOP-DOWN, completely seamless pullover sweater features a geometric color work pattern around the body and cuff and stripes on the shoulders and back. This sweater's unusual top-down construction includes set-in sleeve caps that are worked at the same time as the rest of the shoulder. This unusual construction allows for the stripes to be perfectly matched and is also a lot of fun to work! The pieces of the shoulder are done in sections that grow from pick-up stitches, which helps to add a bit of extra structure right where it is needed most.

FINISHED SIZE

About 30¼ (33½, 37½, 41¾, 46)" (77 [85, 95, 106, 117] cm) bust circumference.

Pullover shown measures 33½" (85 cm).

YARN

Sport Weight (#2 Fine)

Shown here: Blue Sky Alpacas Alpaca Silk (50% alpaca, 50% silk; 146 yd [133 m]/50 g): #110 Ecru (A), 4 (5, 6, 6, 7) skeins; #123 Ruby (B), 1 (1, 1, 1, 2) skeins; #137 Sapphire (C), 2 (2, 3, 3, 3) skeins.

NEEDLES

Size U.S. 5 (3.75 mm): 24" (61 cm) circular (cir) and set of 4 or 5 double-pointed (dpn).

Adjust needle size if necessary to obtain the correct gauge.

NOTIONS

Stitch markers (m)

Stitch holders or waste yarn

Yarn needle

GAUGE

23 sts and 25 rnds = 4" (10 cm) in St st.

The sweater begins by working a wide panel that spans across the back of the shoulders. Then, two narrow panels are added for the fronts at the cast-on edges of the shoulders. Stitches for the sleeve caps are picked up along the selvedge edges of the back and fronts, and the fronts, sleeve caps, and back are worked together down to the underarm. The sleeve stitches are divided out, and the body is worked straight with no shaping in a colorwork pattern. Then the sleeves are worked from the top down, allowing for easy length adjustment. Finally, stitches are picked up for the ribbing at the collar. Then you can congratulate yourself for creating a totally seamless garment that requires no sewing whatsoever!

While working the sections that are knitted flat, carry the unused stripe colors along at the selvedge edge by twisting them together with the color of yarn you are about use. This will keep the strands nice and neat, and greatly reduce the number of ends to weave in. Similarly, at the beginning of every round, twist the unused colors of yarn together with the color you are about to use.

Back

With cir and color A (A, B, A, A), CO 34 (36, 40, 42, 44) sts for back neck. Do not join; work back and forth in rows.

Beg on Row 4 (10, 6, 3, 11) of Stripe Patt and work as foll:

Shape Shoulders

Sizes 41¾ (46)" only:

SET-UP ROW (WS): Purl to end, use the backward loop method (see Techniques) to CO 2 sts—44 (46) sts.

All Sizes:

ROW 1 (RS): Knit to end, use the backward loop method (see Techniques) to CO 2 sts—2 sts inc'd.

ROW 2 (WS): Purl to end, use the backward loop method to CO 2 —2 sts inc'd.

Rep the last 2 rows 8 (9, 9, 9, 10) times—70 (76, 80, 84, 90) sts.

Sizes 41¾ (46)" only:

NEXT ROW (RS): Knit to end, use the backward loop method (see Techniques) to CO 2 sts—86 (92) sts.

All Sizes:

Knit 7 (7, 9, 8, 8) rows even, ending after WS Row 4 (12, 10, 8, 6) of Stripe Patt.

Break yarns. Place all onto a st holder or waste yarn.

Right Front

Rotate back so CO edge is at the top, with RS facing. With cir and color C (B, C, B, A), beg at right edge, pick up and knit 22 (24, 25, 26, 28) sts along right shoulder edge (picking up 1 st in each shoulder CO st, plus 4 (4, 5, 4, 4) sts between the CO sts).

Beg on WS Row 12 (6, 12, 6, 2) of Stripe Patt.

Work 17 (19, 23, 27, 29) rows even, ending after WS Row 4 (12, 10, 8, 6) of Stripe Patt.

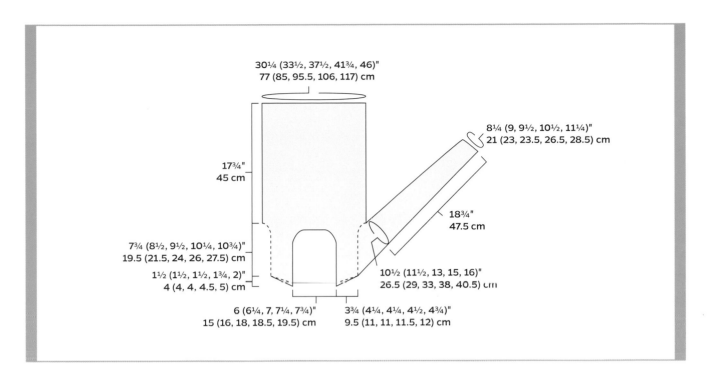

30¼ (33½, 37½, 41¾, 46)"
77 (85, 95.5, 106, 117) cm

8¼ (9, 9½, 10½, 11¼)"
21 (23, 23.5, 26.5, 28.5) cm

17¾"
45 cm

18¾"
47.5 cm

7¾ (8½, 9½, 10¼, 10¾)"
19.5 (21.5, 24, 26, 27.5) cm

1½ (1½, 1½, 1¾, 2)"
4 (4, 4, 4.5, 5) cm

10½ (11½, 13, 15, 16)"
26.5 (29, 33, 38, 40.5) cm

6 (6¼, 7, 7¼, 7¾)"
15 (16, 18, 18.5, 19.5) cm

3¾ (4¼, 4¼, 4½, 4¾)"
9.5 (11, 11, 11.5, 12) cm

Break yarns Place all sts onto a st holder or waste yarn.

Left Front

With RS of back facing, cir and color C (B, C, B, A), beg at neck edge of left shoulder, pick up and knit 22 (24, 25, 26, 28) sts along left shoulder edge (picking up 1 st in each shoulder CO st, plus 4 (4, 5, 4, 4) sts between the CO sts).

Beg on Row 12 (6, 12, 6, 2) of Stripe Patt.

Work 17 (19, 23, 27, 29) rows even, ending after WS Row 4 (12, 10, 8, 6) of Stripe Patt. Do not break yarn.

Yoke

Cont working in Stripe Patt, beg with RS Row 5 (1, 11, 9, 7), and work as foll:

JOINING ROW (RS): Work 22 (24, 25, 26, 28) left front sts, pm, pick up and knit 24 (26, 28, 30, 32) sts along the selvedge edges of the left front and back for the left sleeve, return 70 (76, 80, 86, 92) held back sts onto the

empty end of the cir with RS facing, pm, knit across back sts, pm, pick up and knit 24 (26, 28, 30, 32) sts along the selvedge edges of the back and right front for right sleeve, return 22 (24, 25, 26, 28) held right front sts onto the empty tip of the cir with RS facing, pm, knit to end of right front sts—162 (176, 186, 198, 212) sts; 22 (24, 25, 26, 28) sts each front, 24 (26, 28, 30, 32) sts each sleeve, and 70 (76, 80, 86, 92) sts for back.

Shape Sleeve Cap

SLEEVE INC ROW (WS): *Purl to m, sl m, M1P, purl to next m, M1P, sl m; rep from * once more, purl to end—4 sts inc'd.

SLEEVE INC ROW (RS): *Knit to m, sl m, M1, knit to next m, M1, sl m; rep from * once more, knit to end—4 sts inc'd.

Rep the last 2 rows 0 (0, 0, 1, 1) time— 170 (184, 194, 214, 228) sts; 22 (24, 25, 26, 28) sts each front, 28 (30, 32, 38, 40) sts each sleeve, and 70 (76, 80, 86, 92) sts for back. [Ends after Row 7 (3, 1, 1, 11) of Stripe Patt.]

Purl 1 WS row.

Work Sleeve Inc Row on RS.

Rep the last 2 rows 1 (1, 1, 2, 2) times—178 (192, 202, 226, 240) sts, 22 (24, 25, 26, 28) sts each front, 32 (34, 36, 44, 46) sts each sleeve, and 70 (76, 80, 86, 92) sts for back. [Ends after Row 11 (7, 5, 7, 5) of Stripe Patt]

Work 3 rows even in Stripe Patt.

Work Sleeve Inc Row on RS.

Rep the last 4 rows 3 (4, 3, 0, 0) times 194 (212, 218, 230, 244) sts; 22 (24, 25, 26, 28) sts each front, 40 (44, 44, 46, 48) sts each sleeve, and 70 (76, 80, 86, 92) sts for back. [Ends after Row 3 (3, 9, 11, 9) of Stripe Patt]

Shape Front Neck and Sleeve Caps

Work 3 rows even in Stripe Patt.

NECK AND SLEEVE INC ROW (RS): K1, M1, *knit to m, sl m, M1, knit to next m, M1, sl m; rep from * once more, knit to last st, M1, k1—6 sts inc'd.

Rep the last 4 rows 0 (0, 0, 2, 1) times—200 (218, 224, 248, 256) sts;

23 (25, 26, 29, 30) sts each front, 42 (46, 46, 52, 52) sts each sleeve, and 70 (76, 80, 86, 92) sts for back. *[Ends after Row 7 (7, 1, 11, 5) of Stripe Patt]*

Shape Front Neck, Body, and Sleeve Caps

Sizes 30¼ (46)" only:

Work 3 rows even in Stripe Patt.

NECK, BODY AND SLEEVE INC ROW (RS): K1, M1, *knit to 1 st before m, M1, k1, sl m, M1, knit to next m, M1, sl m, k1, M1; rep from * once more, knit to last st, M1, k1—210 (266) sts; 25 (32) sts each front, 44 (54) sts each sleeve, and 72 (94) sts for back. *[Ends after Row 11 (9) of Stripe Patt]*

All Sizes:

Purl 1 WS row.

BODY AND SLEEVE INC ROW (RS): *Knit to 1 st before m M1, k1, sl m, M1, knit to next m, M1, sl m, k1, M1; rep from * once more, knit to end—8 sts inc'd.

Purl 1 WS row.

NECK, BODY, AND SLEEVE INC ROW (RS): K1, M1, *knit to 1 st before next m, M1, k1, sl m, M1, knit to next m, M1, sl m, k1, M1; rep from * once more, knit to last st, M1, k1—10 sts inc'd.

Rep the last 4 rows 1 (2, 2, 2, 2) times—246 (272, 278, 302, 320) sts; 31 (34, 35, 38, 41) sts each front, 52 (58, 58, 64, 66) sts each sleeve, and 80 (88, 92, 98, 106) sts for back. *[Ends after Row 7 (7, 1, 11, 9) of Stripe Patt]*

Sizes 37½ (41¾, 46)" only:

Purl 1 WS row.

Rep Body and Sleeve Inc Row—286 (310, 328) sts; 36 (39, 42) sts each front, 60 (66, 68) sts each sleeve, and 94 (100, 108) sts for back. *[Ends after Row 3 (1, 11) of Stripe Patt.]*

Join Neck and Divide Body and Sleeves

Sizes 30¼ (33½) only:

Break yarn for all colors. With RS facing, sl all the left front sts before the m to the right needle, remove m, sl all the sts before the next m onto a st holder or waste yarn for the left sleeve, keep the m in place to indicate the beg of rnd. Beg of rnd is at the left underarm.

DIVIDE SLEEVES AND JOIN NECK RND: Join yarn and cont with the Stripe Patt as est, k80 (88) back sts to the next m (right back), remove m, sl 52 (58) sleeve sts onto a st holder or waste yarn for the right sleeve, remove m, use the backward loop method to CO 7 (8) sts for underarm, knit 31 (34) right front sts, use the backward loop method to CO 18 (20) sts for front neck, join to work in the rnd, being careful not to twist work, knit 31 (34) left front sts to held sts, use the backward loop method to CO 7 (8) sts for underarm—174 (192) sts. *[Ends after Rnd 8 of Stripe Patt.]*

Sizes 37½ (41¾, 46)" only:

Break yarn for all colors. With RS facing, sl all the left front sts before the first m to the right needle, sl m, sl all the sleeve sts before the second m to the right needle, sl m. This m indicates the new beg of rnd; it is at the left back.

JOIN NECK RND: Join yarn and cont with the Stripe Patt as est, k94 (100, 108) back sts, sl m, k60 (66, 68)

CHART A

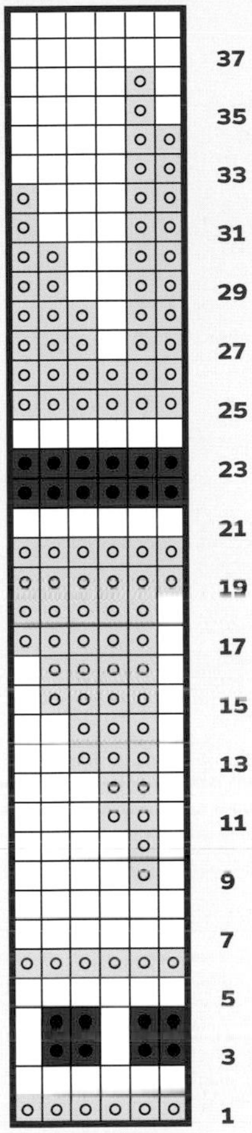
37
35
33
31
29
27
25
23
21
19
17
15
13
11
9
7
5
3
1

CHART B

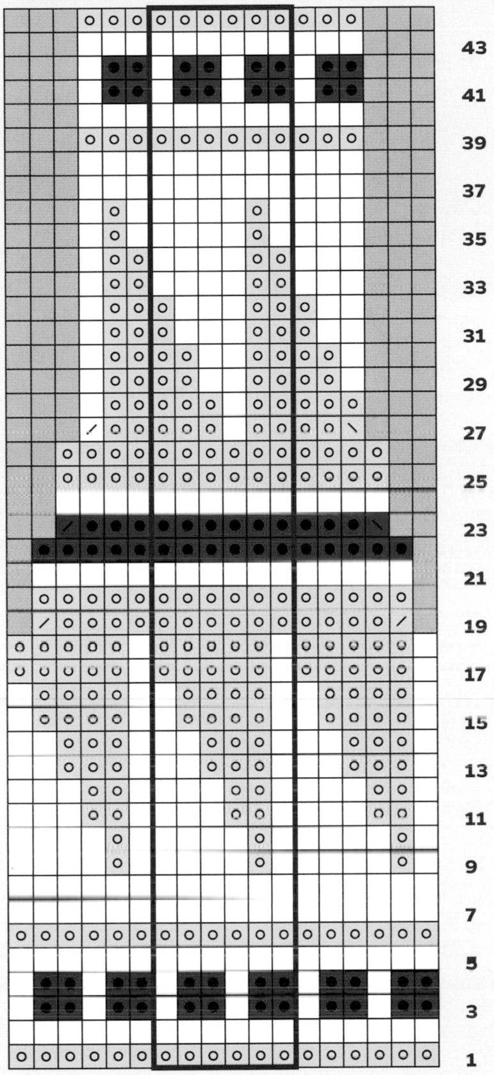
43
41
39
37
35
33
31
29
27
25
23
21
19
17
15
13
11
9
7
5
3
1

STRIPE PATTERN

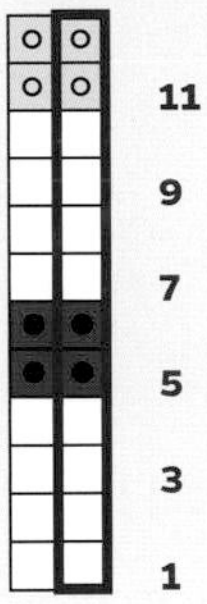
11
9
7
5
3
1

- with color A knit on RS, purl on WS
- with color C knit on RS, purl on WS
- with color B knit on RS, purl on WS
- k2tog in indicated color
- ssk in indicated color
- no stitch
- pattern repeat

sleeve sts, sl m, k36 (39, 42) right front sts, use the backward loop method to CO 22 (22, 24) sts for front neck, join to work in the rnd being careful not to twist work, k60 (66, 68) left front sts, sl m, 60 (66, 68) sleeve sts to end of rnd—308 (332, 352) sts; 36 (39, 42) sts each sleeve, 94 (100, 108) sts each front and back. [Ends after Rnd 4 (2, 12) of Stripe Patt]

BODY AND SLEEVE INC RND: *K1, M1, knit to 1 st before next m, M1, k1, sl m, M1 knit to next m, M1, sl m; rep from * once more—8 sts inc'd.

Knit 1 rnd.

Rep the last 2 rnds 0 (1, 2) times, then work Body and Sleeve Inc Rnd once more—324 (356, 384) sts; 64 (72, 76) sts each sleeve, 98 (106, 116) sts each back and front. [Ends after Rnd 7 of Stripe Patt]

DIVIDE BODY AND SLEEVE RND: Knit 98 (106, 116) back sts, remove m, sl 64 (72, 76) sleeve sts onto a st holder or waste yarn for right sleeve, remove m, use the backward loop method to CO 10 (14, 16) sts for underarm; rep from * once more for front and left sleeve, pm for beg of rnd—216 (240, 264) sts. ()Ends after Rnd 8 of Stripe Patt.)

Body

All Sizes:
Cont working in Stripe Patt for 2 rnds, until Rnd 10 is completed.

Work Rnds 1–38 from Chart A 2 times. Then work Rnds 1–23 once more.

Break yarn for colors B and C. Cont working with color A only as foll:

Size 30¼" only:
INC RND: Knit, inc 2 sts evenly around—176 sts.

Sizes 33½ (37½, 41¾, 46)" only:
Knit 1 rnd.

All Sizes:
EST RIBBING: *K2, p2; rep from *.

Cont working as est for 1½" (3.8 cm).

BO very loosely, using a larger needle held in your right hand if necessary.

Sleeve

Return 52 (58, 64, 72, 76) held sts from one sleeve onto dpn. With an empty dpn and color A, beg at center of underarm CO sts, pick up and knit 4 (4, 5, 7, 8) sts, knit to the end of held sts, then pick up and knit 4 (4, 5, 7, 8) sts from the last half of the CO sts—60 (66, 74, 86, 92) sts. [Ends after Rnd 9 of Stripe Patt]

Cont working the Stripe Patt as est while working as foll:

Sizes 30¼ (33½)" only:
Knit 8 rnds in Stripe Patt, ending after Rnd 5 of patt.

Shape Sleeve

All Sizes:
DEC RND: Ssk, knit to last 2 sts, k2tog—2 sts dec'd.

Knit 7 (7, 7, 5, 5) rnds in Stripe Patt.

Rep the last 8 (8, 8, 6, 6) rnds 4 (4, 5, 8, 8) times, then work Dec Rnd once more—48 (54, 60, 66, 72) sts. [Ends after Rnd 10 (10, 10, 4, 4) of Stripe Patt]

Knit 12 (12, 12, 6, 6) rnds in Stripe Patt, ending after Rnd 10 of patt. (Piece should meas about 9¾, 25 cm) from underarm.)

Sizes 30¼ (33½)" only:
Work Rows 1–38 from Chart A, then rows 1–6 from Chart A.

Sizes 37½ (41¾, 46)" only:
Work Rows 1–44 from Chart B—54 (60, 66) sts rem.

All Sizes:
Break yarn for color B and C. Cont working with color A only as foll:

Sizes 33½ (37½, 46)" only:
Rep Dec Rnd—52 (52, 64) sts rem.

Sizes 30¼ (41¾)" only:
Knit 1 rnd.

All Sizes:
Est Ribbing: *K2, p2; rep from *.

Cont working as est for 2" (5 cm).

BO very loosely, using a larger needle held in your right hand if necessary. Work second sleeve the same as the first.

Finishing
Block to measurements.

Neck Edging
With cir and color A, beg at right edge of back-neck CO sts, pick up and knit 34 (36, 40, 42, 44) sts along the back neck CO sts, 30 (32, 31, 32, 32) sts along the selvedge edge of the left front, 18 (20, 22, 22, 24) sts from the front-neck CO sts, 30 (32, 31, 32, 32) sts along the selvedge edge of the right front, pm for beg of rnd and join to work in the rnd—112 (120, 124, 128, 132) sts.

EST RIBBING: *K2, p2; rep from *.

Cont working as est for 1¼" (3.2 cm).

BO loosely in rib.

Weave in ends.

danio hat

THIS CUTE LITTLE CAP is simple to make and uses only one skein of yarn. The folded-up flaps are held in place by decorative buttons at each side, giving this simple cap cute, quirky character and a pop of graphic color.

FINISHED SIZE

18¾ (20½, 22¼)" (47.5 [52, 56.5] cm) circumference at brim. 8" (20.5 cm) tall. Select a size slightly smaller than your head circumference for the best fit.

Hat shown measures 20½" (52 cm)

YARN

Chunky Weight (#5 Bulky)

Shown here: Cascade Yarns Baby Alpaca Chunky (100% baby alpaca, 108 yd [99 m]/100 g): #565 Natural, 1 skein.

NEEDLES

Size U.S. 10 (6 mm): 16" (40.5 cm) circular (cir) and set of 4 double-pointed (dpn).

Adjust needle size if necessary to obtain the correct gauge.

NOTIONS

Stitch markers (m)

Thin contrasting color yarn or thread (about 12" [30.5 cm] long).

Stitch holder or waste yarn

Tapestry needle

Two 1" (2.5 cm) buttons

Matching thread and sewing needle for button

GAUGE

14 sts and 22 rnds = 4" (10 cm) in St st.

13 sts and 26 rnds = 4" (10 cm) in Seed st.

Notes

The hat is knitted seamlessly from the top down on double-pointed needles. The folded brim is worked in two parts with 8 overlapping stitches on each side.

Beginning a top-down circular hat can be a bit awkward. To make it as easy as possible, use the backward loop method for the M1 increases. In other words, make a backward loop on your right thumb and pass it to your right needle as if to cast on. Be careful to make your loop firm so that a hole does not appear below your increase.

Crown

Use the long-tail method (see Techniques) to CO 6 sts onto a dpn, leaving a tail about 10" (25.5 cm) long. You'll use this tail to close the hole at the top of the hat later.

INC ROW: *K1, M1; rep from * to last st, k1, CO 1 using the backward loop method (see Techniques)—12 sts.

Distribute the 12 sts evenly over 3 dpn. Place marker (pm) for beg of rnd and join to work in the rnd.

Shape Crown

Note: *Change to cir needle when sts no longer fit comfortably on dpn.*

SET-UP RND: *K1, M1, pm, k1; rep from *—18 sts.

Knit 1 rnd.

INC RND: *Knit to m, M1, sl m; rep from * to last st, k1—6 sts inc'd.

Rep the last 2 rnds 7 (8, 9) times— 66 (72, 78) sts; 11, (12, 13) sts between markers.

NEXT RND: Knit, removing all m except beg of rnd m.

Cont working in St st (knit all sts, every rnd) until piece meas 7¾" (19.5 cm) from CO.

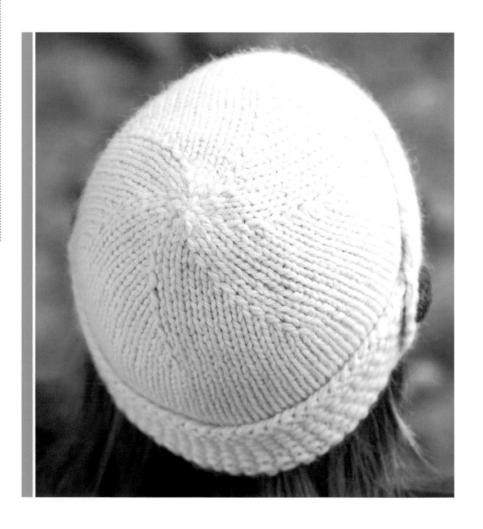

Weaving in Chunky Ends

Weaving in ends invisibly can be challenging, especially when you're working with a very thick yarn. The large gauge exaggerates thickened stitches, and big chunky ends poking out can make your work look sloppy. If your yarn has more than one ply, then you are in luck! All you need to do is separate the plies in two parts. Weaving each ply into the fabric separately will give you a much more invisible result.

Knitted Covered Buttons

Making your own buttons is so much fun and adds a special touch to your finished project. I've done it all, from dyeing store-bought buttons to sculpting toggles out of porcelain clay, but I think the easiest method is to use a covered button kit. I stock up in a variety of sizes whenever I make it out to the fabric store.

For the buttons on this hat, I used a 1⅜" (3.5 cm) half ball covered button set made by Dritz. I knitted a tiny circle using the template on the back of the package with yarn from an old project. I selected a fine yarn and knitted at a tight gauge to keep the metal backing from showing between my stitches as much as possible. The package instructs you to stretch the fabric over the top of the button, catching the edges on the teeth on the underside of the button. If you try this, be careful not to stretch your knitted fabric too much, as the backing will show through (unless that's what you want!). Then it's as simple as snapping the back plate into place.

Brim

The brim is worked flat in 2 sections.

Flap 1

SET-UP ROW (RS): K8. With a tapestry needle, run a length of waste yarn through the previous 8 sts under your needle, keeping the sts on the knitting needle; k33 (36, 39), run a second length of waste yarn through the previous 8 sts under your needle, keeping the sts on the knitting needle; put the rem 25 (28, 31) unworked sts on a st holder or another piece of waste yarn—41 (44, 47) sts rem.

Work in Seed st for 8 rows, ending after a RS row.

Shape Flap:

DEC ROW (WS): P2tog, work in Seed st to last 2 sts, ssp—2 sts dec'd.

DEC ROW (RS): Ssk, work in Seed st to the last 2 sts, k2tog—2 sts dec'd.

Rep the last 2 rows once more— 33 (36, 39) sts rem.

BIND-OFF ROW (WS): P2tog, bind off loosely pwise to last 2 sts, ssp, pass the second stitch on the right needle over the first, break yarn, and fasten off the last st.

Flap 2

Hold hat to beg at the right edge of the held sts. Using the waste yarn as a guide, pick up and knit 8 sts before the held sts, remove waste yarn, place the 25 (28, 31) held sts on an empty needle, and knit to end, pick up and knit 8 sts using the waste yarn as your guide, remove waste yarn—41 (44, 47) sts.

Cont working same as Flap 1.

Finishing

Thread the tail from CO onto a tapestry needle, run the needle through each CO st to cinch the top of the hat closed. Weave in all the ends (see sidebar). If desired, lightly block the hat to smooth out the sts. Fold the flaps up and sew a button to each side where the flaps overlap. The buttons should be all you need to secure the flaps, but if your yarn is particularly slippery, it may be necessary to sew the flaps down.

finch cardigan

THIS EASY CROPPED CARDIGAN was described by one of my editors as "delightfully retro," though I think this piece has a decidedly modern appeal. The cropped length and single button make this a practical staple that looks great with anything. Flat construction and minimal shaping make this piece ideal for first-time sweater knitters.

FINISHED SIZE

31 (35½, 39½, 43, 47½)" (79 [90, 100.5, 109, 120.5] cm) bust circumference.

Cardigan shown measures 35½" (90 cm).

YARN

Chunky Weight (#5 Bulky)

Shown here: Cascade Yarns Baby Alpaca Chunky (100% baby alpaca; 108 yd [99 m]/100 g): #596 Mocha (A), 1 (1, 2, 2, 2) skeins; #573 Lemon Yellow (B), 3 (4, 4, 5, 5) skeins.

NEEDLES

Size U.S. 10 (6 mm): straight and 24" (61 cm) circular (cir).

Adjust needle size if necessary to obtain the correct gauge.

NOTIONS

Stitch markers (m)

Tapestry needle

1¼" (3.2 cm) button

Matching thread and needle for button

GAUGE

14 sts and 22 rows = 4" (10 cm) in St st.

16 sts and 24 rows = 4" (10 cm) in k1, p1 ribbing.

Note: Row gauge in St st is important for proper fit of this garment.

Stitch Guide

1-ROW BUTTONHOLE:
Move the yarn to the back of the work, sl the next two sts to the right needle one at a time, pass the first slipped st over the second as if to BO, sl the next st from the left needle to the right, pass the first slipped st over the second as if to BO, slip the remaining sl st back to the left needle, use the backward loop method (see Techniques) to CO 2 sts.

Notes

The body and sleeves are worked flat in one long piece from cuff to cuff, and the edging is added after the body is sewn together. Inverted bust darts are used to obtain the raised front shaping. Sleeve caps are shaped with a modified raglan technique to create a smooth, seamless line from arm to arm across the back.

Right Sleeve

With color A and straight needles, CO 38 (40, 42, 46, 50) sts.

NEXT 10 ROWS: *K1, p1; rep from *.

Break yarn for color A.

Cont with color B as foll:

Work 2 (6, 10, 10, 6) rows in St st (knit on RS, purl on WS), ending after a WS row.

If you desire longer sleeves, add length here.

Shape Sleeve

INC ROW (RS): K1, M1, knit to last st, M1, k1—2 sts inc'd.

Work 7 (5, 3, 3, 3) rows even in St st, ending after a WS row.

Rep the last 8 (6, 4, 4, 4) rows 4 (5, 7, 7, 8) times—48 (52, 58, 62, 68) sts rem.

Knit 1 RS row.

Shape Sleeve Cap

BO 2 sts at beg of next 2 (4, 6, 6, 8) rows, then BO 3 sts at beg of the foll 6 rows—26 (26, 28, 32, 34) sts rem.

Break yarn, but leave the sts on the needle.

Right Body

Use cir, color B, and the backward loop method (see Techniques) to CO 32 (34, 34, 33, 33) sts for body, with WS of right sleeve sts facing, p26 (26, 28, 32, 34) right sleeve sts, then use the backward loop method to CO 32 (34, 34, 33, 33) sts—90 (94, 96, 98, 100) sts. Do not join; work back and forth in rows.

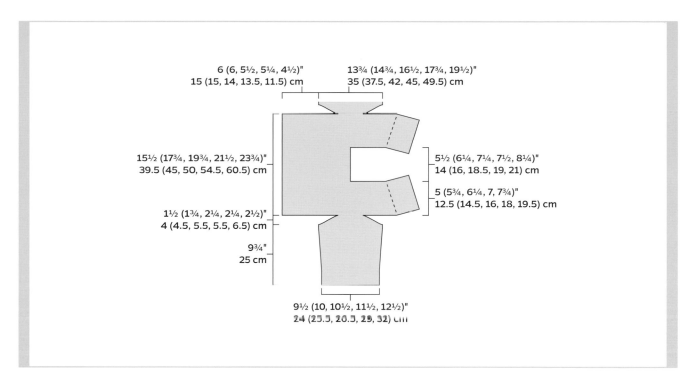

6 (6, 5½, 5¼, 4½)"
15 (15, 14, 13.5, 11.5) cm

13¾ (14¾, 16½, 17¾, 19½)"
35 (37.5, 42, 45, 49.5) cm

15½ (17¾, 19¾, 21½, 23¾)"
39.5 (45, 50, 54.5, 60.5) cm

5½ (6¼, 7¼, 7½, 8¼)"
14 (16, 18.5, 19, 21) cm

5 (5¾, 6¼, 7, 7¾)"
12.5 (14.5, 16, 18, 19.5) cm

1½ (1¾, 2¼, 2¼, 2½)"
4 (4.5, 5.5, 5.5, 6.5) cm

9¾"
25 cm

9½ (10, 10½, 11½, 12½)"
24 (25.5, 26.5, 29, 32) cm

Shape Bust

SET-UP ROW (RS): K15, place marker (pm) for bust shaping, knit to end.

Work 3 rows even in St st, ending after a WS row.

DEC ROW (RS): Knit to m, sl m, ssk, knit to end—1 st dec'd.

Rep the last 4 rows 4 (5, 5, 6, 6) times—85 (88, 90, 91, 93) sts rem.

Work even in St st for 5 (5, 9, 9, 13) rows, ending after a WS row.

(Piece should meas 5 (5¾, 6¼, 7, 7¾)" (12.5 [14.5, 16, 18, 19.5] cm) from the CO edge of the right body.)

Center Back

NEXT ROW (RS): BO 40 (41, 42, 42, 43) sts for front, knit to the end—45 (47, 48, 49, 50) sts rem for back.

Work even in St st until the piece meas 10½ (12, 13½, 14½, 16)" (26.5 [30.5, 34.5, 37, 40.5] cm) from the CO edge of the right body, ending after a RS row.

Left Body

NEXT ROW (WS): Purl to end, use the backward loop method to CO 40 (41, 42, 42, 43) sts for left front—85 (88, 90, 91, 93) sts.

Work 3 (3, 7, 7, 11) rows in St st, ending after a RS row.

Shape Bust

SET-UP ROW (WS): P70 (73, 75, 76, 78), pm, purl to end.

INC ROW (RS): Knit to m, sl m, k1, M1, knit to end—1 st inc'd.

Work 3 rows even in St st, ending after a WS row.

Rep the last 4 rows 4 (5, 5, 6, 6) times—90 (94, 96, 98, 100) sts.

Work 2 rows even in St st, ending after a WS row.

(Piece should meas 5 (5¾, 6¼, 7, 7¾)" (12.5 [14.5, 16, 18, 19.5] cm) from the CO edge of the left body.)

NEXT ROW (RS): BO 32 (34, 34, 33, 33) sts, k26 (26, 28, 32, 34), BO rem 32 (34, 34, 33, 33) sts, and break yarn.

Left Sleeve

Join color B, preparing to work a WS row.

Shape Sleeve Cap

Use the backward loop method to CO 3 sts at the end of the next 6 rows, then CO 2 sts at end of the foll 2 (4, 6, 6, 8) rows—48 (52, 58, 62, 68) sts.

Shape Sleeve

Work 7 (5, 3, 3, 3) rows even in St st, ending after a WS row.

DEC ROW (RS): Ssk, knit to last 2 sts, k2tog—2 sts dec'd.

Rep the last 8 (6, 4, 4, 4) rows 4 (5, 7, 7, 8) times—38 (40, 40, 46, 50) sts rem.

Work 2 (6, 10, 10, 6) rows even in St st, ending after a RS row. Adjust sleeve length here, if desired. Break

yarn for color B. Cont working with color A.

Purl 1 WS row.

NEXT 9 ROWS: *K1, p1; rep from *.

BO very loosely in rib.

Finishing

Block piece to measurements.

Sew the angled part at the top of the sleeves to the sides of the body using

Tips for Mattress Stitch

The mattress stitch (see Techniques) is a very useful seaming technique that every knitter should master. It can be worked on all manner of seams: vertical, diagonal, horizontal, or even curved. When the mattress stitch is done properly, the resulting seam blends beautifully with knitted fabrics, and can even be completely invisible, depending on the yarn.

1. Preparing the Fabric:
Some patterns will specify if you need to block the fabric before or after seaming, but there is often a gray area. Use your judgment to determine the order. If you are seaming 2 pieces that are floppy or prone to curling, blocking before seaming will make the process much easier.

2. Arranging Your Pieces:
Mattress stitch is worked with pieces lying flat before you, the right sides facing up, and with the edges that will be sewn together butted up against each other. It's best to map out your seam before you begin. Try to identify points that should align, like the top of a shoulder point, or even just a halfway or quarter mark. Put a little marker at each of these points on both pieces of fabric. They will act as your guide as you seam.

3. Threading Your Needle:
Use a blunt-tipped tapestry needle, and thread it with a long length of yarn. If your yarn is very fuzzy or coarse, and your seam is very long, you may need to use several lengths of yarn and seam in sections.

Whenever possible, you want to use the ends that are already on the knitted fabric. When I know there will be a seam, I always try to leave long tails when I cast on or bind off. This reduces the number of ends to weave in, and helps the edge to look smoother. See the Techniques section at the end of this book for more of my tips about the mattress stitch.

---

the mattress stitch (each of these seams should be 3½ (3¾, 4¼, 4¼, 4¾)" (8.5 [9.5, 11, 11, 12] cm) long.) Starting at the lower edge, sew the front to the back at the sides using the mattress stitch (each of these seams should be 6 (6, 5½, 5¼, 4½)" (15 [15, 14, 13.5, 11.5] cm) long). Cont sewing the sleeve seam from underarm to cuff.

Front Edging

With the RS facing, use cir and color A, beg at lower edge of right front, pick up and knit 40 (41, 42, 42, 43) sts along the right front edge up to the back neck, 20 (22, 24, 28, 32) sts along the back neck, then 40 (41, 42, 42, 43) sts along the left-front edge—100 (104, 108, 112, 118) sts.

NEXT 9 ROWS: *K1, p1; rep from *.

BO very loosely in rib.

Lower Edging

With the RS facing, use cir and color A, beg at lower edge of front edging at left front, pick up and knit 8 sts along the side of the front edging, 21 (23, 26, 30, 32) sts along the left front lower edge, 62 (68, 78, 88, 96) sts along lower edge of back, 21 (23, 26, 30, 32) sts along lower edge of right front, then 8 sts along the edge of the front edging—120 (130, 146, 164, 176) sts.

NEXT 7 ROWS: *K1, p1; rep from *.

BUTTONHOLE ROW (RS): Work in rib as est to last 8 sts, work a 1-row buttonhole (see Stitch Guide), work to end as est.

NEXT 7 ROWS: *K1, p1; rep from *.

BO very loosely in rib.

Sew the button to the left front, being careful to align it with the buttonhole on the right front.

Weave in ends. Lightly block the seams and edging so they lie flat.

bowerbird
wrap

LOOSE GAUGE AND CABLES make for a light, squishy wrap with a lot of visual interest. Cables are worked over a 1 × 1 rib stitch pattern for a completely reversible fabric. The design is finished with a quirky twisted cord fringe on either end.

FINISHED SIZE
About 13¼" (33.5 cm) wide and 62½" (159 cm) long.

YARN
DK Weight (#3 Light)

Shown here: Malabrigo Silky Merino (50% silk, 50% baby merino wool; 150 yd [137 m]/50 g): #431 Tatami (A), #63 Natural (B), #406 Narciso (C), 2 skeins each.

NEEDLES
Size U.S. 11 (8 mm): straight

Adjust needle size if necessary to obtain the correct gauge.

NOTIONS
Cable needle

Crochet hook to attach tassels

Stitch markers (m) (optional)

GAUGE
24 sts and 18 rows = 4" (10 cm) in Cable Patt.

Stitch Guide
Cable Pattern (multiple of 32 sts + 16):
(also, see chart)

ROWS 1–9: *K1, p1; rep from *.

ROW 10 (RS): *[K1, p1] 8 times, sl 8 sts to cn and hold in front, [k1, p1] 4 times, [k1, p1] 4 times from cn; rep from * once more, [k1, p1] to end.

ROWS 11–19: Rep Row 1.

ROW 20 (RS): Sl 8 sts to cn and hold in front, [k1, p1] 4 times, [k1, p1] 4 times from cn, *[k1, p1] 8 times, sl 8 sts to cn and hold in front, [k1, p1] 4 times, [k1, p1] 4 times from cn; rep from * once more.

Rep Rows 1–20 for patt.

> ### Note
> *You may find it helpful to place a stitch marker every 16 stitches to separate the cable-cross sections.*

Scarf
With color A, CO 80 sts.

EST RIBBING (RS): *K1, p1; rep from *.

Work Rows 1–20 of Cable Patt 2 times.

Change to color B, work Rows 1–20 of Cable Patt 2 times.

Change to color C, work Rows 1–20 of Cable Patt 2 times.

Change to color B, work Rows 1–20 of Cable Patt 2 times.

Change to color A, work Rows 1–20 of Cable Patt 2 times.

Change to color B, work Rows 1–20 of Cable Patt 2 times.

Change to color C, work Rows 1–20 of Cable Patt 2 times.

BO all sts very loosely in rib.

Finishing
Weave in the loose ends as invisibly as possible. Block piece to measurements, pulling the cables out horizontally to accentuate them. Don't move the scarf until it is completely dry. Attach 14 twisted cord tassels to each end using the directions on the following page.

CABLE CHART

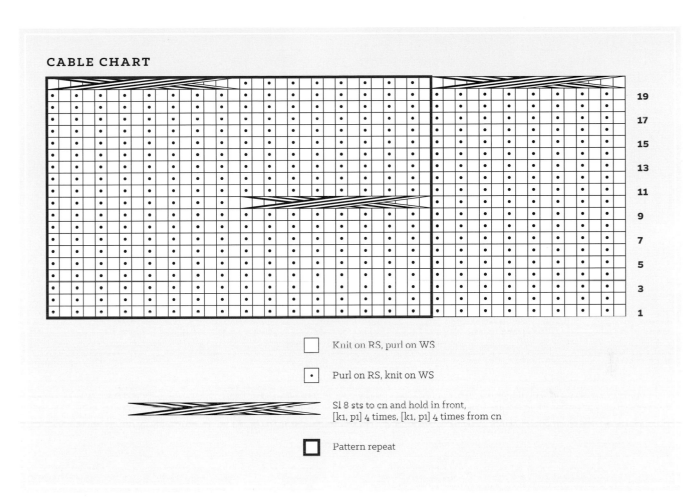

☐ Knit on RS, purl on WS

• Purl on RS, knit on WS

Sl 8 sts to cn and hold in front,
[k1, p1] 4 times, [k1, p1] 4 times from cn

☐ Pattern repeat

Twisted Cord Fringe

1 Cut 2 lengths of yarn 12" (30.5 cm) long. Hold 2 strands together, and fold them in half to make a loop.

2 Locate where you want your fringe, and use a crochet hook to pull the loop through the scarf. Pull the loop up about 1" (2.5 cm).

3 Bring the tail through the loop and pull it tight (Figure 1).

4 Twist each fringe:

A. Divide each fringe into halves.

B. Twist the right half between your fingers, twisting toward the right until the cord is very tight and wants to twist back on itself, but keep it straight. For a very tight cord, twist as hard as the yarn will allow without bunching up.

C. Hold the twisted half in your right hand, and hold the untwisted half in the left. Twist the 2 strands together by bringing the right strand over the top of the left strand, and then back under to its original position. Continue twisting the strands in this manner to the end.

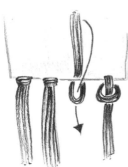

Figure 1

D. Holding the ends together, tie an overhand knot to secure the twist. Trim the ends so they are even.

engle cardigan

THIS LIGHT, AIRY CARDIGAN has a fluttering draped front that is both feminine and elegant. Wear it open with the collar flipped up, or fold the collar down and close the front with a sweater pin. The modular construction shows off the beautiful ombre effect of the surprisingly light and airy Austermann Murano Lace yarn. The cardigan is knitted in every which direction with minimal seams (just at the shoulders), making this a very entertaining project.

FINISHED SIZE

About 31 (35¼, 38½, 43¾, 48)" (79 [89.5, 98, 111, 122] cm) bust circumference.

Cardigan shown measures 35¼" (89.5 cm).

YARN

Worsted Weight (#4 Medium)

Shown here: Austermann Murano Lace (53% wool, 47% acrylic; 437 yd [400 m]/100 g): #004, 3 (3, 3, 3, 4) skeins.

Note: If you are particular about knitting symmetrical ombre striped sleeves, buy an extra skein of yarn.

NEEDLES

Size U.S. 9 (5.5 mm): 24" and 40" (60 and 100 cm) circular (cir) and set of 4 or 5 wooden double-pointed (dpn).

Note: Wooden needles are recommended because the suggested yarn is slippery and wooden needles are less prone to sliding out of the stitches.

Adjust needle size if necessary to obtain the correct gauge.

NOTIONS

4 removable markers

2 stitch markers (m)

Stitch holders or waste yarn

Tapestry needle

GAUGE

15 sts and 21 rows = 4" (10 cm) in St st.

Notes

The cardigan is knitted in one piece with minimal seams. The body begins at the lower edge (which will be the waist after the edging is worked), and is worked upward toward the underarm where it is divided for the back and front. The back and fronts are worked separately to the shoulder. The shoulders are seamed, then stitches for the sleeve are picked up around the armhole edge. Sleeves are worked from the top down by picking up stitches around the armhole, working short-rows to form the sleeve cap, and then continuing down the sleeve working circularly. Working from the top down allows for easy length and circumference adjustment, so try the sleeve on periodically to test the fit. Stitches for the edging are picked up along fronts and lower body, and the edging is knit from the body out. Collar stitches are picked up around the neck and edging edges.

Body

With shorter cir, CO 62 (76, 90, 96, 110) sts. Place a removable marker into the first and last sts. You will use these later to pick up sts for the edging. Do not join; work back and forth in rows.

Shape Front Edges

Purl 1 WS row.

EDGE INC ROW (RS): K1, M1, knit to last st, M1, k1—2 sts inc'd.

Rep the last 2 rows 4 times—72 (86, 100, 106, 120) sts.

Shape Darts

SET-UP ROW (WS): P22 (27, 33, 34, 39) for left front, pm, p28 (32, 34, 38, 42) for back, pm, purl to end for right front.

DART AND EDGE INC ROW (RS): K1, M1, knit to m, M1, sl m, knit to next m, sl m, M1, knit to last st, M1, k1—4 sts inc'd.

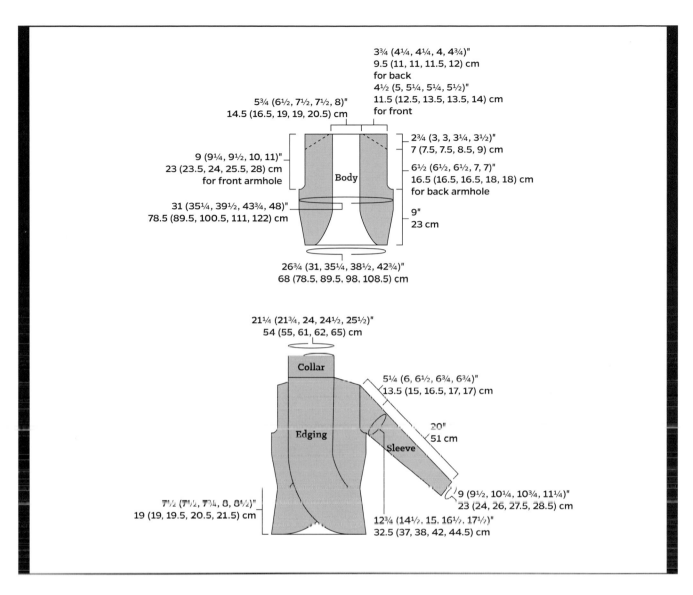

3¾ (4¼, 4¼, 4, 4¾)"
9.5 (11, 11, 11.5, 12) cm
for back
4½ (5, 5¼, 5¼, 5½)"
11.5 (12.5, 13.5, 13.5, 14) cm
for front

5¾ (6½, 7½, 7½, 8)"
14.5 (16.5, 19, 19, 20.5) cm

2¾ (3, 3, 3¼, 3½)"
7 (7.5, 7.5, 8.5, 9) cm

9 (9¼, 9½, 10, 11)"
23 (23.5, 24, 25.5, 28) cm
for front armhole

6½ (6½, 6½, 7, 7)"
16.5 (16.5, 16.5, 18, 18) cm
for back armhole

Body

31 (35¼, 39½, 43¾, 48)"
78.5 (89.5, 100.5, 111, 122) cm

9"
23 cm

26¾ (31, 35¼, 38½, 42¾)"
68 (78.5, 89.5, 98, 108.5) cm

21¼ (21¾, 24, 24½, 25½)"
54 (55, 61, 62, 65) cm

Collar

5¼ (6, 6½, 6¾, 6¾)"
13.5 (15, 16.5, 17, 17) cm

Edging

20"
51 cm

Sleeve

7½ (7½, 7¾, 8, 8½)"
19 (19, 19.5, 20.5, 21.5) cm

9 (9½, 10¼, 10¾, 11¼)"
23 (24, 26, 27.5, 28.5) cm

12¾ (14½, 15, 16½, 17½)"
32.5 (37, 38, 42, 44.5) cm

[Purl 1 WS row, work Edge Inc Row] 2 times.

Purl 1 WS row.

Rep the last 6 rows 2 (2, 2, 3, 3) times, then work Dart and Edge Inc Row once more—100 (114, 128, 142, 156) sts; 32 (37, 43, 47, 52) sts outside the markers, 36 (40, 42, 48, 52) sts between the markers. Remove dart markers on the next row.

Place another removable marker into the first and last sts. You will use these later to pick up sts for the edging.

Cont working even in St st (knit on RS, purl on WS) until piece meas 9" (23 cm) from CO, ending after a RS row. Break yarn, but leave the sts on needle.

Divide For Armholes

With the WS facing, put the next 19 (22, 25, 27, 29) sts on a holder for the right front, then the next 4 (4, 4, 6, 8) sts on a separate holder for underarm, join yarn and p54 (62, 70, 76, 82) sts for back, put the next 4 (4, 4, 6, 8) sts on a holder for underarm, then put the last 19 (22, 25, 27, 29) sts on a separate holder for left front—54 (62, 70, 76, 82) rem for back.

Back

Shape Armholes

DEC ROW (RS): K1, ssk, knit to last 3 sts, k2tog, k1—2 sts dec'd.

Purl 1 WS row.

Rep the last 2 rows 1 (2, 4, 6, 7) times—50 (56, 60, 62, 66) sts rem.

Work even until piece meas 6½ (6½, 6½, 7, 7)" (16.5 [16.5, 16.5, 18, 18] cm) from divide, ending after a WS row.

Shape Shoulders

DEC ROW 1 (RS): K1, ssk, knit to last 3 sts, k2tog, k1—2 sts dec'd.

DEC ROW 2 (WS): P1, p2tog, purl to last 3 sts, ssp, p1—2 sts dec'd.

Rep the last 2 rows 6 (7, 7, 7, 8) times—22 (24, 28, 30, 30) sts rem.

Size 43¾" only:

DEC ROW 1 (RS): K1, ssk, knit to last 3 sts, k2tog, k1—28 sts rem.

All Sizes:

BO all sts loosely.

Right Front

> **Note:** *If you're using an ombre yarn, refer to the sidebar titled "Symmetrical Ombre Stripes" (see page 51).*

Return the 19 (22, 25, 27, 29) held right front sts onto needle and join yarn preparing to work a WS row.

Shape Armhole

Purl 1 WS row.

DEC ROW (RS): Knit to last 3 sts, k2tog, k1—1 st dec'd.

Rep the last 2 rows 1 (2, 4, 6, 7) times—17 (19, 20, 20, 21) sts rem.

Work even in St st until armhole meas 9 (9¼, 10, 10, 11)" (23 [23.5, 25.5, 25.5, 28] cm) from divide, ending after a WS row.

BO all sts loosely.

Left Front Panel

Return the 19 (22, 25, 27, 29) held left front sts onto needle and join yarn preparing to work a WS row.

Shape Armhole

Purl 1 WS row.

DEC ROW (RS): K1, ssk, knit to end—1 st dec'd.

Shape Cap with Short-Rows (see Techniques)

SHORT-ROW 1: K32 (36, 38, 42, 44), w&t; p16 (18, 19, 21, 22), w&t—15 (17, 18, 20, 21) sts rem unwrapped at each end of rnd.

SHORT-ROW 2: Knit to wrapped st from previous row, knit that st leaving the wrap intact, w&t; purl to the wrapped st from the previous row, purl that st leaving the wrap intact, w&t.

Rep the last short-row 12 (14, 15, 16, 16) more times—2 (2, 2, 3, 4) sts rem unwrapped at each end of rnd.

NEXT ROW (RS): Knit to end of rnd.

Shape Sleeve

Knit 12 (9, 9, 7, 6) rnds.

DEC RND: Ssk, knit to last 2 sts, k2tog—2 sts dec'd.

Rep the last 13 (10, 10, 8, 7) rnds 6 (8, 8, 10, 11) times—34 (36, 38, 40, 42) sts rem.

Work even in St st (knit all sts, every rnd) until the sleeve meas 18½" (47 cm) from underarm.

[Purl 2 rnds, knit 2 rnds] 3 times.

Purl 2 rnds.

BO loosely pwise.

Work second sleeve the same as the first.

Rep the last 2 rows 1 (2, 4, 6, 7) times—17 (19, 20, 20, 21) sts rem.

Work even in St st until the armhole meas 9 (9¼, 10, 10, 11)" (23 [23.5, 25.5, 25.5, 28] cm) from divide, ending after a WS row.

BO all sts loosely.

Block to measurements, being careful that the armhole edges are neatly blocked to prepare for picking up sts for the sleeves.

Sew the shoulder seams using the mattress stitch, aligning the slanted edges of the back with the flat BO edges at the top of the fronts and easing the extra sts from the front shoulder evenly across the back shoulder.

Sleeve

Note: Because the front shoulder piece is longer than the back, the shoulder seam is not exactly at the top of the shoulder. Be careful to pick up stitches evenly.

With RS facing and dpn, beg at the center of the underarm, k2 (2, 2, 3, 4) held underarm sts, pick up and knit 44 (50, 52, 56, 58) sts evenly around the armhole, knit the rem 2 (2, 2, 3, 4) held underarm sts. Pm for beg of rnd and join to work in the rnd—48 (54, 56, 62, 66) sts.

Edging

With longest cir and RS facing, beg at left front shoulder seam, pick up and knit 50 (52, 54, 50, 54) sts evenly along the edge to the m, pm, pick up and knit 26 (26, 26, 32, 32) along the diagonal edge to the next m, pm, pick up and knit 1 st for each of the 62 (76, 90, 96, 110) CO sts along the bottom edge to next m, pm, pick up and knit 26 (26, 26, 32, 32) along the diagonal edge to the next m, pm, pick up and knit 50 (52, 54, 50, 54) sts along the straight edge to the right front shoulder seam—214 (232, 250, 260, 282) sts. Do not join; work back and forth in rows. Circular needle is used to accommodate large number of sts.

Work 11 rows even in St st, ending after a WS row.

Shape Edging

INC ROW 1 (RS): *Knit to m, sl m, [k1, M1] to next m, sl m; rep from * once more, knit to end—266 (284, 302, 324, 346) sts.

Work 11 (11, 13, 15, 17) rows even in St st, ending after a WS row.

Place a removable m into the first and last st of the row. You will use these later when picking up sts for the collar.

NEXT ROW (RS): Purl.

NEXT ROW (WS): Knit.

Work 4 rows even in St st, ending after a RS row.

NEXT ROW (RS): Purl.

NEXT ROW (WS): Knit.

INC ROW 2 (RS): *Knit to m, sl m, [k2, M1] to the second m, sl m; rep from *

Symmetrical Ombre Stripes

I selected an ombre yarn for this design to show off the interesting modular construction. While this beautiful yarn becomes more fun to knit as each stripe gradually develops, these stripes also present a particular challenge: How do you make the left and right sides look the same?

Some ombre yarns follow a predictable pattern, and it's easy to pick up where the pattern left off as you begin a new section, while others (like this brand) seem to march to another beat.

In this design, there are two points where you should try to match the ombre stripes. The first is when you begin knitting each of the fronts. Examine your ball of yarn to see if the color of the ombre stripe will cause a sharp line where you will join the new ball. If the colors don't match, unwind the ball until they do.

If you're a perfectionist, you can try to observe the progression of the ombre deeper into the ball of yarn to see if it will change to the correct color of stripe as you knit the second section.

The other point where you should try to match the ombre is the second sleeve. Compare all your balls of yarn before you begin the sleeves. If you see two balls that appear to have a similar rhythm to their ombre, use one for the left sleeve and the other for the right. Remember, if you see the stripes aren't turning out like you expected, it's perfectly legal to break yarn in the middle and unwind the ball until you find the sweet spot.

once more, knit to end—318 (336, 354, 388, 410) sts.

Work 3 rows even in St st, ending after a WS row.

NEXT ROW (RS): Purl.

NEXT ROW (WS): Knit.

NEXT ROW (RS): Knit.

NEXT ROW (WS): Purl.

Rep the last 4 rows 2 times.

NEXT ROW (RS): Purl.

NEXT ROW (WS): Knit.

BO very loosely pwise.

Collar

With cir and WS facing (pick up with the WS facing so when the collar is turned the pick-up ridge is hidden), beg at corner of left front edging, pick up and knit 13 sts between the corner and the m, remove m, pick up and knit 16 (16, 18, 19, 20) sts along the side of the edging to the shoulder seam, pick up and knit 1 st for each of the 22 (24, 28, 28, 30) BO back neck sts, pick up and knit 16 (16, 18, 19, 20) sts along the side of the edging to the m, remove m, pick up and knit 13 sts between the m and the corner of the edging—80 (82, 90, 92, 96) sts.

ROW 1 (WS): Knit.

ROW 2 (RS): Purl.

ROW 3 (WS): Purl.

ROW 4 (RS): Knit.

ROW 5 (WS): Purl.

ROW 6 (RS): Knit.

Rep the last 6 rows once more.

NEXT ROW (WS): Knit.

NEXT ROW (RS): Purl.

NEXT ROW (WS): Purl.

NEXT ROW (RS): Knit.

Rep the last 4 rows 2 times.

NEXT ROW (WS): Knit.

NEXT ROW (RS): Purl.

BO loosely kwise.

Finishing

Weave in the loose ends. Wet-block the cardigan and arrange it to dry with the back facing up. Use pins or blocking wires to pull the edging outward into a semicircular arrangement, carefully stretching the welted edgings so they lie flat and the BO edges make a smooth line. Let it dry completely before you move it.

woodstar
beret

THIS FAIR ISLE BERET features an eye-catching geometric color work motif in three colors. The hat is worked from a chart, with integrated crown shaping, which forms a pretty seven-pointed star at the top. The hat coordinates with the Woodstar Mitts (see page 56).

FINISHED SIZE
About 18¼" (46.5 cm) circumference at brim, 23¼" (59 cm) circumference at widest part.

YARN
Sport Weight (#2 Fine)

Shown here: Berroco Ultra Alpaca Light (50% alpaca, 50% wool; 144 yd [132 m]/50 g): #4201 Winter White (A), #42104 Briny Deep (B), and #4275 Pea Soup Mix (C), 1 skein each.

NEEDLES
Size U.S. 4 (3.5 mm): 16" (40 cm) circular (cir) and set of 4 or 5 double-pointed (dpn).

Adjust needle size if necessary to obtain the correct gauge.

NOTIONS
Stitch markers (m)

Yarn needle

GAUGE
21 sts = 4" (10 cm) in k2, p2 ribbing

24 sts and 30 rnds = 4" (10 cm) in Colorwork Chart.

Notes

Securing Long Floats: *There are several places in the colorwork pattern where the unused color of yarn is carried for more than 5 stitches. You must secure these long floats on the back side. To do this, knit about 4 stitches with the used color, then simply twist the 2 colors together before you begin knitting the next stitch, then continue with the pattern as charted.*

You may find it helpful to place a marker between each pattern repeat to make it easier to keep track of where you are in each row.

To minimize loose ends, carry the unused color up by twisting it together with the used colors before working the last st of each rnd.

Make-One Increase (M1): *For the best-looking result, make a backward loop on your right thumb and transfer it to your right needle as if to cast on a stitch.*

Hat

With color A and cir, CO 96 sts. Pm for beg of rnd and join to work in the rnd, being careful not to twist sts.

NEXT 9 RNDS: *K2, p2; rep from *.

INC RND: With color B, k8, *M1, k2; rep from *—140 sts.

Work Rnds 1–52 from Colorwork Chart changing to dpn when sts no longer fit comfortably on cir—21 sts rem.

Break yarn for colors A and C, work 2 rnds even in color B. Break yarn for B leaving a 12" (30.5 cm) tail. Thread the tail onto a yarn needle, and pull through the rem sts and cinch the top closed. Thread the needle around once more, and secure the end to the WS.

Finishing

Weave in all the loose ends. Wet-block the hat over a plate or Frisbee with about 29" (73.5 cm) circumference (about 9" [23 cm] diameter). Pull the brim toward the center into the smallest ring the form will allow. Let the hat dry completely before moving.

COLORWORK CHART

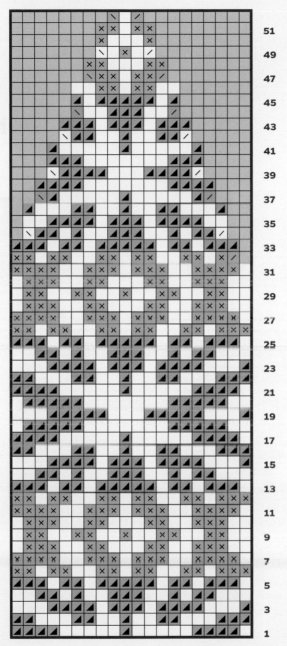

☐	with color A, knit
◣	with color B, knit
✕	with color C, knit
╱	k2tog in indicated color
╲	ssk in indicated color
▨	no stitch
☐	pattern repeat

woodstar
mitts

THESE FAIR ISLE MITTS feature a cheerful geometric color work motif. Fingerless mitts are a great transition accessory for when it's not quite cold enough outside to warrant gloves. I have also been known to wear mine in the summer at the office, when the air conditioner is blasting! The color work motif coordinates with the Woodstar Beret (see page 52).

FINISHED SIZE

About 18¼" (46.5 cm) circumference at brim, 23¼" (59 cm) circumference at widest part.

YARN

Sport Weight (#2 Fine)

Shown here: Berroco Ultra Alpaca Light (50% alpaca, 50% wool; 144 yd [132 m]/50 g): #4201 Winter White (A), #42104 Briny Deep (B), and #4275 Pea Soup Mix (C), 1 skein each.

NEEDLES

Size U.S. 4 (3.5 mm): 16" (40 cm) circular (cir) and set of 4 or 5 double-pointed (dpn).

Adjust needle size if necessary to obtain the correct gauge.

NOTIONS

Stitch markers (m)

Yarn needle

GAUGE

24 sts and 30 rnds = 4" (10 cm) in Colorwork Chart.

Notes

Securing Long Floats: *There are several places in the Colorwork Chart where the unused color of yarn is carried for more than 5 sts. You must secure these long floats on the back side. To do this, knit about 4 sts with the specified color of yarn, then simply twist the 2 colors of yarn together before you beg knitting the next st, then cont with the patt as charted.*

To minimize loose ends, carry the unused color up by twisting it together with the used colors before *working the last stitch of each round. Carrying the yarn along in this position will prevent holes from forming around the increases for the thumb gusset later.*

Cuff

With color A CO 42 sts. Divide sts evenly over 3 or 4 dpn. Pm for beg of rnd and join to work in the rnd being careful not to twist sts.

NEXT 3 RNDS: *K1, p1; rep from *.

NEXT RND: Sl 1 st pwise wyb, join B, knit to the end with color B.

Work Rnds 1–18 from Colorwork Chart.

Thumb Gusset

Work Rnds 19–38 from Colorwork Chart, increasing for thumb gusset as charted—56 sts.

Divide Thumb Gusset

Work Rnd 39 of Colorwork Chart as follows: Put the first 16 sts on a st holder or waste yarn, use the backward loop method (see Techniques) to CO 1 with color A

then CO 1 with color B as indicated in chart with a + symbol, cont working to end of rnd as charted—42 sts rem.

Hand

Work Rnds 40–47 from Colorwork Chart.

NEXT RND: Sl 1 pwise wyb, knit to the end with color C.

Knit 1 rnd with color A.

NEXT 2 RNDS: *K1, p1; rep from *.

BO loosely in rib.

Thumb

Return 16 held thumb sts to 2 dpn. With color B and a third dpn pick up

and knit 4 sts evenly from the gap inside the thumb, knit to end of row—20 sts. Pm for beg of rnd.

Break yarn for color B.

DEC RND: With color A, k2tog, knit to last 2 sts, ssk—18 sts rem.

NEXT 3 RNDS: *K1, p1; rep from *.

BO in rib.

Make a second mitt the same as the first.

Finishing

Weave in the loose ends and wet-block to smooth out the colorwork.

COLORWORK CHART

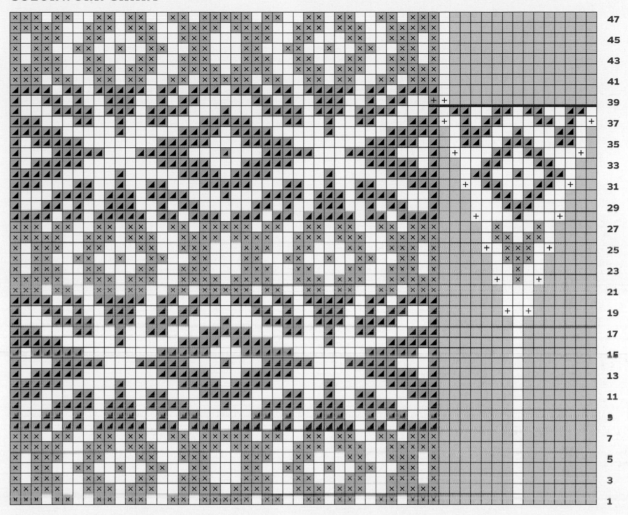

47
45
43
41
39
37
35
33
31
29
27
25
23
21
19
17
15
13
11
9
7
5
3
1

☐ with color A, knit

◢ with color B, knit

⊠ with color C, knit

➕ use the backwards loop method to CO 1 st

▨ no stitch

━ Place 16 sts onto st holder or waste yarn

barbet
turtleneck

THIS EASY RAGLAN PULLOVER is not only stylish but also a great first sweater project for an inexperienced knitter. The sweater is entirely reversible, knitted from the top down, and totally seamless. Strategically placed colorblock sections have a slimming effect that flatters all body types. The top-down construction allows for easy length adjustment, and it makes for a more successful sweater, especially for a first time sweater knitter.

FINISHED SIZE
About 34 (39, 43, 47, 51)" (86.5 [99, 109, 119.5, 129.5] cm) bust circumference.

Turtleneck shown measures 39" (99 cm).

YARN
Worsted weight (#4 Medium)

Shown here: Berroco Vintage (50% acrylic, 40% wool, 10% nylon; 217 yd [198 m]/100 g): #5180 Dried Plum (A), 3 (3, 4, 4, 4) skeins; #5107 Cracked Pepper (B), 3 (3, 3, 3, 4) skeins.

NEEDLES
Size U.S. 10 (6 mm). 24" (60 cm) circular (cir) and set of 4 or 5 double-pointed (dpn).

Adjust needle size if necessary to obtain the correct gauge.

NOTIONS
Stitch markers (m)

Stitch holder or waste yarn

Yarn needle

GAUGE
16 sts and 24 rnds = 4" (10 cm) in St st.

17 sts and 26 rnds = 4" (10 cm) in Waffle Rib.

Stitch Guide

Waffle Rib Collar Pattern (multiple of 2 sts):
(worked with WS facing)

RND 1: *K1, p1; rep from *.

RND 2: Purl.

Rep Rnds 1 and 2 for patt.

Lower Waffle Rib Pattern (multiple of 2 sts):

RND 1: *K1, p1; rep from *.

RND 2: Knit.

Rep Rnds 1 and 2 for patt.

Notes

The sweater is begun by knitting the turtleneck collar. From the base of the collar, stitches are increased to form the raglan shaping around the shoulders. Then, the sleeves are divided out, and the body is knitted with some gentle waist and hip shaping. The sleeves are worked last, with gradual decreases down to the wrist.

Collar

Note: The turtleneck collar is worked with the WS facing as you knit because it will be folded over when the garment is worn. The last 2" (5 cm) of the collar is worked in a reversible ribbing pattern that serves two functions: to draw in the collar at the neck and to make a nicer transition between the collar and the body of the sweater where the WS might peek out.

With color A and cir, CO 104 (108, 112, 112, 116) sts. Place marker (pm) for beg of rnd and join to work in the rnd, being careful not to twist sts.

Work 11 rnds in the Waffle Rib Collar Patt, ending after Rnd 1 of patt.

Break yarn for color A. Join color B and cont working Waffle Rib Collar Patt until piece meas 6¼" (16 cm) from CO, ending after Rnd 2 of patt.

EST RIBBING: *K1, p1; rep from *.

Cont working in ribbing as est until piece meas 8" (20.5 cm) from CO.

Yoke

SET-UP RND: *K18 (16, 16, 14, 14) for sleeve, pm, k34 (38, 40, 42, 44) for body, pm; rep from * once more.

Shape Raglan

INC RND: *Kfb, knit to 1 st before the next m, kfb, sl m; rep from * 3 more times—8 sts inc'd.

Knit 1 rnd.

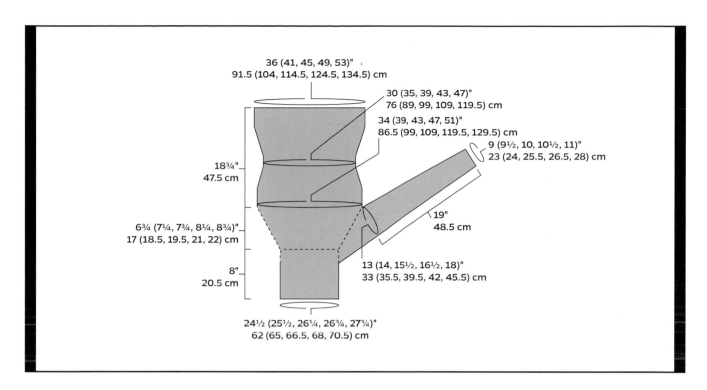

36 (41, 45, 49, 53)"
91.5 (104, 114.5, 124.5, 134.5) cm

30 (35, 39, 43, 47)"
76 (89, 99, 109, 119.5) cm

34 (39, 43, 47, 51)"
86.5 (99, 109, 119.5, 129.5) cm

9 (9½, 10, 10½, 11)"
23 (24, 25.5, 26.5, 28) cm

18¾"
47.5 cm

19"
48.5 cm

6¾ (7¼, 7¾, 8¼, 8¾)"
17 (18.5, 19.5, 21, 22) cm

13 (14, 15½, 16½, 18)"
33 (35.5, 39.5, 42, 45.5) cm

8"
20.5 cm

24½ (25½, 26¼, 26¾, 27¾)"
62 (65, 66.5, 68, 70.5) cm

Rep the last 2 rnds 13 (15, 18, 20, 23) times—216 (236, 264, 280, 308) sts; 46 (48, 54, 56, 62) sts each sleeve and 62 (70, 78, 84, 92) sts each back and front.

Work even in St st (knit all sts, every rnd) until piece meas 6¾ (7¼, 7¾, 8¼, 8¾)" (17 [18.5, 19.5, 21, 22] cm) from the turtleneck collar. Be sure to take this meas in an area that does not cross any of the raglan inc's.

Divide Body and Sleeves

NEXT RND: *Put 46 (48, 54, 56, 62) sleeve sts onto a st holder or waste yarn, remove m, use the backward loop method (see Techniques) to CO 6 (8, 8, 10, 10) sts for underarm, k62 (70, 78, 84, 92) to next m, remove m; rep from * once more keeping beg of rnd m in place—136 (156, 172, 188, 204) sts rem.

Body

Knit 18 rnds

Shape Waist

SET-UP RND: K20 (23, 25, 28, 30), pm, k34 (40, 44, 48, 52), pm, k34 (38, 42, 46, 50), pm, k34 (40, 44, 48, 52), pm, k14 (15, 17, 18, 20) sts.

DEC RND: *Knit to 2 sts before m, k2tog, sl m, knit to next m, sl m, ssk; rep from * once more, knit to end—4 sts dec'd.

Knit 5 rnds.

Rep Dec Rnd—128 (148, 164, 180, 196) sts.

NEXT RND: K3 (4, 4, 5, 5), break yarn for B, join color A and knit to end.

Knit 4 rnds.

[Rep Dec Rnd, then knit 5 rnds] 2 times—120 (140, 156, 172, 188) sts rem.

Knit 5 rnds.

INC RND: *Knit to m, M1, sl m, knit to next m, sl m, M1, rep from * once more, knit to end—4 sts inc'd.

Rep the last 6 rnds 5 times—144 (164, 180, 196, 212) sts.

Cont working even in St st until piece meas 14½" (37 cm) from divide.

Edging

Work in Lower Waffle Rib Patt for 2" (5 cm), ending after Rnd 1 of patt.

BO loosely kwise.

Sleeve

Return 46 (48, 54, 56, 62) held sts from one sleeve onto 3 dpn. With color B and an empty dpn, beg at center of underarm, pick up and knit 3 (4, 4, 5, 5) sts from the CO edge, knit to end of held sts, pick up and knit 3 (4, 4, 5, 5) sts from rem CO edge—52 (56, 62, 66, 72) sts. Pm for beg of rnd.

Knit 9 rnds.

Shape Sleeve

> **Note:** Read the following instructions before cont; color changes before sleeve shaping is completed.

DEC RND: Ssk, knit to last 2 sts, k2tog—2 sts dec'd.

Knit 10 (9, 7, 6, 5) rnds.

Rep the last 11 (10, 8, 7, 6) rnds 7 (8, 10, 11, 13) times—36 (38, 40, 42, 44) sts remain; *and at the same time*, when sleeve meas 4½" (11.5 cm) from underarm, break yarn for B and change to color A for remainder of sleeve.

Cont working even in St st until sleeve meas 17" (43 cm) from underarm.

Keeping Your Markers Straight

Designers use markers because they really simplify pattern directions. They save knitters from a lot of counting. Sometimes a pattern tells you to use what seems to be an excessive number of markers. It can be confusing to keep all the instructions straight for each marker, especially if you're working in rounds. I have a few tricks that can help you keep it all straight.

For example, I might use 2 markers right next to each other to indicate the beginning of rounds, so I don't get that marker confused with any other marker.

I also like to take advantage of the different colors and sizes of markers that usually come in a package. If I'm always supposed to M1 before the next marker, I might make that one red to indicate "stop, M1 before passing." Then if I'm always supposed to K2tog after the next marker, I might make that one green to indicate "pass m, then K2tog."

In the waist and hip shaping sections of my Barbet pattern, there are 5 markers in use: one to indicate the beginning of the round, 2 on the front, and 2 on the back. If you read ahead in the pattern, which I recommend you always do, you'll see that the increases and decreases are worked on the outside of each pair of markers. To make it easier to quickly see where I am in my round, I used large purple markers for the front and small green markers for the back. That way, I always know to leave the stitches between the pairs of markers alone.

Edging

Work the Lower Waffle Rib Patt for 2" (5 cm), ending after Rnd 1 of patt.

BO loosely kwise.

Finishing

Weave in loose ends, using the ends around the underarm to close up any holes that may occur around the picked-up stitches there. Block to finished measurements.

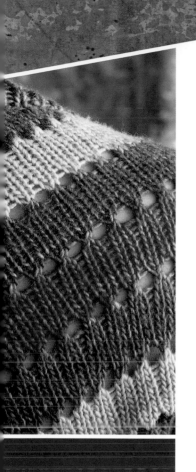

tanager shrug

THIS EYE-CATCHING BOLERO features a bold stripe pattern that accentuates the bias knit fabric and its unusual construction. A row of eyelets between each stripe adds a delicate texture to break up the heavy stripes.

FINISHED SIZE
About 30 (35, 41, 45, 53)" (76 [89, 104, 114.5, 134.5] cm) bust circumference.

Shrug shown measures 35" (89 cm).

YARN
DK Weight (#3 Light)

Shown here: Malabrigo Silky Merino (51% silk, 49% merino wool, 150 yd [137 m]/50 g). #402 Hot Pink (A), 1 skein; #430 Smoke (B), 1 (2, 2, 2, 2) skeins; #429 Cape Cod Gray (C), 1 skein.

NEEDLES
Size U.S. 8 (5 mm): 32" (80 cm) circular (cir) and double-pointed (dpn).

Adjust needle size if necessary to obtain the correct gauge.

NOTIONS
Stitch markers (m)

Yarn needle

Waste yarn for holding stitches

GAUGE
16 sts and 29 rows = 4" (10 cm) in Gauge Patt.

Back Neck

With color A and cir, CO 5 sts.

SET-UP ROW (RS): [Kfb] twice, pm, [kfb] twice, k1—9 sts.

INC ROW (WS): Pfb, purl to last 2 sts, pfb, p1—2 sts inc'd.

INC ROW (RS): Kfb, knit to 1 st before m, kfb, sl m, kfb, knit to last 2 sts, kfb, k1—4 sts inc'd.

Rep the last 2 rows 0 (0, 0, 1, 2) times, then work Inc Row on WS once more—17 (17, 17, 23, 29) sts; 8 (8, 8, 11, 14) sts at beg of RS row before m, 9 (9, 9, 12, 15) sts at end of RS row after m.

Break yarn for color A.

COLOR-CHANGE INC ROW (RS): Join color B, k1 (1, 1, 2, 1), yo, k1, [yo, k2tog] to m, yo, sl m, k1, [yo, k2tog] to last 2 (2, 2, 3, 2) sts, yo, k1, yo, k1 (1, 1, 2, 1)—21 (21, 21, 27, 33) sts.

[Work Inc Row on WS then Inc Row on RS] 4 times, then work Inc Row on WS once more—47 (47, 47, 53, 59) sts; 23 (23, 23, 26, 29) sts at beg of RS row before m, 24 (24, 24, 27, 30) sts at end of RS row after m.

Break yarn for color B.

Body

Note: *The body is worked by casting on stitches to each edge of the neck. These cast-on stitches make the edges that lie across the front of the shoulders. The front and back are worked at the same time in one long row that reaches from the left shoulder front to the center of the back and back again to the right shoulder front. When the length for the back piece is reached, the left and right shoulders are separated to form the lower edge of the shrug.*

Notes

Circular needle is used to accommodate large number of sts. Do not join; work back and forth in rows.

The body is worked flat from the top down, beg at the back of the neck. The stripe pattern is shaped into a chevron by using a central increase down the middle of the back. The body is blocked flat before the seams are sewn and the edging is attached.

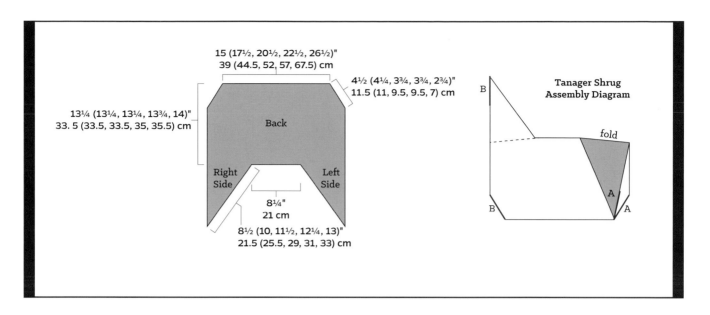

15 (17½, 20½, 22½, 26½)"
39 (44.5, 52, 57, 67.5) cm

4½ (4¼, 3¾, 3¾, 2¾)"
11.5 (11, 9.5, 9.5, 7) cm

13¼ (13¼, 13¼, 13¾, 14)"
33. 5 (33.5, 33.5, 35, 35.5) cm

Back

Right
Side

Left
Side

8¼"
21 cm

8½ (10, 11½, 12¼, 13)"
21.5 (25.5, 29, 31, 33) cm

Tanager Shrug
Assembly Diagram

B

fold

A

B

A

Cast-on Shoulder Stitches

Note: Decreases at the edges paired with increases in the center create the chevron stripe pattern and also keep the stitch count consistent throughout this section.

SET-UP ROW: Prepare to work a RS row. Using the right-hand needle tip and color C use a provisional method (see Techniques) to CO 34 (40, 46, 49, 52) sts for left shoulder, work back neck sts as foll: k1 (1, 1, 2, 1), [yo, k2tog] to m, yo, sl m, k1, [yo, k2tog] to last 1 (1, 1, 2, 1) sts, yo, k1 (1, 1, 2, 1), use a provisional method to CO 34 (40, 46, 49, 52) sts for right shoulder—117 (129, 141, 153, 165) sts.

Work Rows 1–9 of Chevron Patt with color C.

Work Row 10 of Chevron Patt with color B.

Work Rows 1–9 of Chevron Patt with color B.

Work Row 10 of Chevron Patt with color A.

Work Rows 1–9 of Chevron Patt with color A.

Work Row 10 of Chevron Patt with color B.

Work Rows 1–9 of Chevron Patt with color B.

Work Row 10 of Chevron Patt with color C.

Work Rows 1–9 of Chevron Patt with color C.

Work Row 10 of Chevron Patt with color B.

Work Rows 1–5 of Chevron Patt with color B.

Left Side

SET-UP ROW (RS): K2tog, knit to m, remove m, put rem 59 (65, 71, 77, 83) sts onto a st holder or waste yarn—57 (63, 69, 75, 81) sts rem.

DEC ROW (WS): Ssp, purl to end—1 st dec'd.

DEC ROW (RS): K2tog, knit to last 2 sts, ssk—2 sts dec'd.

Work Dec Row on WS once more—53 (59, 65, 71, 77) sts rem.

COLOR-CHANGE DEC ROW 1 (RS). Change to color A, k2tog, [k2tog, yo] to last 3 sts, k1, ssk—51 (57, 63, 69, 75) sts rem.

[Work Dec Row on WS then Dec Row on RS] 4 times, then work Dec Row on WS once more—38 (44, 50, 56, 62) sts rem.

COLOR-CHANGE DEC ROW 2 (RS): Change to color B, k2tog, [k2tog, yo] to last 2 sts, ssk—36 (42, 48, 54, 60) sts rem.

[Work Dec Row on WS then Dec Row on RS] 4 times, then work Dec Row on WS once more—23 (29, 35, 41, 47) sts rem.

Change to color C work Color-Change Dec Row 1—21 (27, 33, 39, 45) sts rem.

[Work Dec Row on WS then Dec Row on RS] 1 (3, 4, 4, 4) times, then work Dec Row on WS 0 (1, 1, 1, 1) more times—18 (17, 20, 26, 32) sts rem.

Sizes 41 (45, 53)" only:

Change to color B and work Color-Change Dec Row 2—18 (24, 30) sts rem.

[Work Dec Row on WS then Dec Row on RS] 1 (3, 4) times—15 (15, 18) sts rem.

Size 53" only:

Work Dec Row on WS—17 sts rem.

Change to color A and work Color-Change Dec Row 1—15 sts rem.

Work Dec Row on WS, then Dec Row on RS, then work Dec Row on WS once more—11 sts rem.

All Sizes:

BO all sts.

Right Side

Return 59 (65, 71, 77, 83) held right side sts onto needle and join color B preparing to work a RS row.

DEC ROW (RS): K2tog, knit to last 2 st, ssk—2 sts dec'd.

DEC ROW (WS): Purl to last 2 sts, p2tog—1 st dec'd.

Rep the last 2 rows once more—53 (59, 65, 71, 77) sts rem.

COLOR-CHANGE DEC ROW 1 (RS): Change to color A, k2tog, [k2tog, yo] to last 3 sts, k1, ssk—51 (57, 63, 69, 75) sts rem.

[Work Dec Row on WS then Dec Row on RS] 4 times, then work Dec Row on WS once more—38 (44, 50, 56, 62) sts rem.

COLOR-CHANGE DEC ROW 2 (RS): Change to color B, k2tog, [k2tog, yo] to last 2 sts, ssk—36 (42, 48, 54, 60) sts rem.

[Work Dec Row on WS then Dec Row on RS] 4 times, then work Dec Row on WS once more—23 (29, 35, 41, 47) sts rem.

Change to color C and work Color-Change Dec Row 1—21 (27, 33, 39, 45) sts rem.

[Work Dec Row on WS then Dec Row on RS] 1 (3, 4, 4, 4) times, then work Dec Row on WS 0 (1, 1, 1, 1) more times—18 (17, 20, 26, 32) sts rem.

Sizes 41 (45, 53)" only:

Change to color B and work Color-Change Dec Row 2—18 (24, 30) sts rem.

[Work Dec Row on WS then Dec Row on RS] 1 (3, 4) times—15 (15, 18) sts rem.

Size 53" only:

Work Dec Row on WS—17 sts rem.

Change to color A and work Color-Change Dec Row 1—15 sts rem.

Work Dec Row on WS, then Dec Row on RS, then work Dec Row on WS once more—11 sts rem.

All Sizes:

BO all sts.

Finishing

Wet-block piece to help the eyelets open up and lie flat. The fabric will naturally grow about 10 to 15 percent when it's wet, but try not to stretch the piece more than that. After the fabric dries completely and has relaxed, it will shrink back a little but will still be about 5 percent bigger than before it was blocked.

After the piece has completely dried, arrange the piece to sew the side seams. Turn the piece so WS is facing. Fold down the points of left and right sides, aligning the tip to the lower corner of the diagonal BO edge as shown in the assembly diagram.

Sew the diagonal BO edge to the straight edge of the corresponding folded side (labeled A and B) in the diagram.

Sleeve Edging

With dpn and color B, beg at the seam, pick up and knit 54 (60, 66, 70, 78) sts evenly around the armhole, Pm for beg of rnd.

NEXT 8 RNDS: *K1, p1; rep from *.

BO loosely in rib.

Front Edging

With cir and color B, beg at the right side seam, pick up and knit 34 (40, 46, 49, 52) sts along the CO edge of the right side, 42 (42, 42, 46, 52) sts along the back neck 34 (40, 46, 49, 52) sts along the CO edge of the left side, 72 (86, 98, 106, 120) sts along the lower edge—182 (208, 232, 250, 276) sts. Pm for beg of rnd.

NEXT 8 RNDS: *K1, p1; rep from *.

BO loosely in rib.

Weave in ends.

orly cardigan

THIS ELEGANT WRAP CARDIGAN features quirky asymmetrical stripes, artfully placed to flatter feminine curves. Lightweight fabric and three-quarter-length sleeves make this a great transitional piece.

FINISHED SIZE

About 29 (33, 36, 40, 44)" (73.5 [84, 91.5, 101.5, 112] cm) bust circumference, tied closed.

Cardigan shown measures 33" (84 cm).

YARN

Fingering Weight (#1 Super Fine)

Shown here: Quince & Co. Finch (100% wool; 221 yd [202 m]/50 g): #105 Glacier (A), 6 (6, 7, 8, 9) skeins; #123 Honey (B), 2 skeins.

NEEDLES

Size U.S 6 (4 mm): 36" (90 cm) circular (cir) and set of 4 or 5 double-pointed (dpn).

Adjust needle size if necessary to obtain the correct gauge.

NOTIONS

Stitch markers (m)

4 removable markers or waste yarn

Stitch holders or waste yarn

Yarn needle

Row counter (optional but highly recommended)

GAUGE

23 sts and 35 rows = 4" (10 cm) in St st.

Stitch Guide

Stripe Pattern (any number of sts):
Note: Keep track of your rows as you work the pattern. The instructions are given with row numbers to make this easier. Work Stripe Patt on the rows specified at the beg of each section.

ROWS 1–4: Color B

ROWS 5–16: Color A

ROWS 17–20: Color B

Work Rows 1–20 for patt, then cont in color A.

Notes

The body is worked flat from the bottom up in 2 pieces: left body and right body. The 2 pieces are joined with a seam that runs the length of the center back. The shoulders are also seamed together, giving the garment some extra structure. Stitches for the sleeve are picked up from around the armhole. The sleeves are worked circularly from the top down for easy length and circumference adjustment. The edging is a simple knitted binding that is worked from picked-up stitches and sewn down on the WS. A knitted i-cord tie is attached to each front at the waist.

Instructions to adjust the length are given in the waist section.

Circular needle is used to accommodate large number of sts. Do not join; work back and forth in rows.

If you adjust the length, the position of the stripes will also need to be considered. The stripes on each sleeve are meant to align with the stripes of the opposite body piece.

Left Body

Note: As you work the instructions below, beg Stripe Patt on Rows 19 and 125. Work all other rows in color A.

With color A and cir, use a provisional method (see Techniques) to CO 76 (93, 105, 121, 136) sts. Do not join; work back and forth in rows.

Shape Front

ROW 1 (RS): Knit to end, use the backward loop method (see Techniques) to CO 2 sts—78 (95, 107, 123, 138) sts.

Rows 2–3 (3, 7, 7, 7)
Purl 1 WS row.

INC ROW (RS): Knit to end, CO 2—2 sts inc'd.

Rep the last 2 rows 0 (0, 2, 2, 2) times—80 (97, 113, 129, 144) sts.

Sizes 29 (33)" only:

Rows 4–13
Purl 1 WS row.

INC ROW (RS): Knit to end, CO 1 st—1 st inc'd.

Rep the last 2 rows 4 times—85 (102) sts.

Shape Hip

All Sizes:

ROW 14 (14, 8, 8, 8) (WS): P18 (29, 35, 45, 54) for front, pm, p52 (56, 60, 64, 68) for side, pm, p15 (17, 18, 20, 22) sts to end for back.

Rows 15 (15, 9, 9, 9)–56 (56, 68, 68, 74)

ROWS 1 AND 3 (FRONT INC, RS): Knit to end, CO 1 st—1 st inc'd.

ROWS 2, 4, AND 6 (WS): Purl.

ROW 5 (HIP DEC AND FRONT INC, RS): Knit to first m, sl m, ssk, knit to 2 sts before the next m, k2tog, sl m, knit to end, CO 1 st—1 st dec'd.

Rep the last 6 rows 6 (6, 9, 9, 10) times—92 (109, 123, 139, 155) sts; 39 (50, 65, 75, 87) sts for front, 38 (42, 40, 44, 46) sts for side, and 15 (17, 18, 20, 22) sts for back.

Rows 57 (57, 69, 69, 75)–80

ROWS 1 AND 3 (RS): Knit.

ROWS 2, 4, AND 6 (WS): Purl.

ROW 5 (HIP DEC AND FRONT INC ROW, RS): Knit to first m, sl m, ssk, knit to 2 sts before the next m, k2tog, sl m, knit to end, CO 1 st—1 st dec'd.

Rep the last 6 rows 3 (3, 1, 1, 0) times—88 (105, 121, 137, 154) sts; 43 (54, 67, 77, 88) sts for front, 30, (34, 36, 40, 44) sts for side, and 15 (17, 18, 20, 22) sts for back.

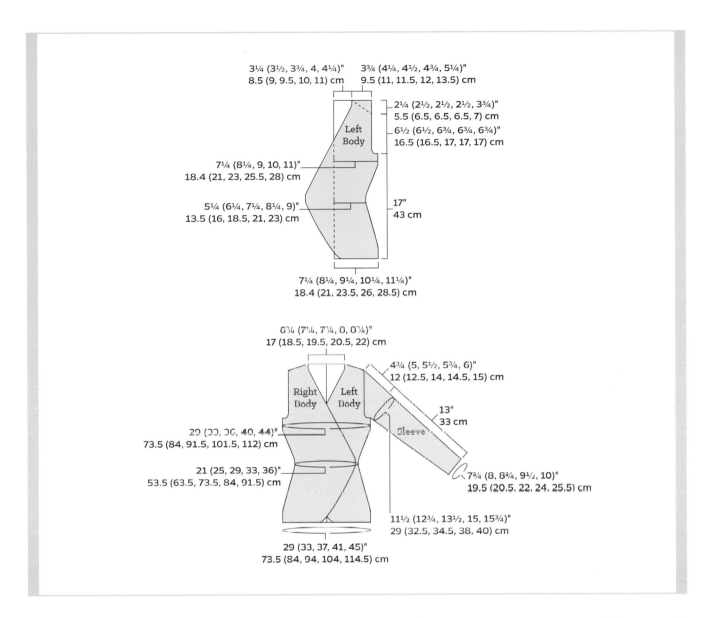

Waist

> **Note:** *To adjust the length here, work a minimum of 2 rows, and end after a WS row.*

ROWS 81–90: Work 10 rows even in St st (knit on RS, purl on WS), ending after a WS row.

Place a removable m into the first and last st of the last row. You'll use the markers when you sew the back seam and apply the front edging.

Shape Bust

Rows 91–98 (106, 122, 126, 134)

ROW 1 (BUST INC, RS): Knit to first m, sl m, M1, knit to next m, M1, sl m, knit to end—2 sts inc'd.

ROW 2 (FRONT DEC, WS): BO 3 sts, purl to end—3 sts dec'd.

ROW 3 (RS): Knit.

ROW 4 (WS): Purl.

Rep the last 4 rows 1 (3, 7, 8, 10) times—86 (101, 113, 128, 143) sts rem; 37 (42, 43, 50, 55) sts for front, 34 (42, 52, 58, 66) sts for side, and 15 (17, 18, 20, 22) sts for back.

Sizes 29 (33, 36, 40)" only:

Rows 99 (107, 123, 127)–110 (122, 130, 134)

ROW 1 (BUST INC, RS): Knit to first m, sl m, M1, knit to next m, M1, sl m, knit to end—2 sts inc'd.

ROW 2 (FRONT DEC, WS): BO 2 sts, purl to end—2 sts dec'd.

ROW 3 (RS): Knit.

ROW 4 (WS): Purl.

Rep the last 4 rows 2 (3, 1, 1) times—86 (101, 113, 128) sts; 31 (34, 39, 46) sts for front, 40 (50, 56, 62) sts for side, and 15 (17, 18, 20) sts for back.

Sizes 29 (33, 36)" only:

Rows 111 (123, 131)–134 (134, 134)

ROW 1 (BUST INC, RS): Knit to first m, sl m, M1, knit to next m, M1, sl m, knit to end—2 sts inc'd.

ROW 2 (FRONT DEC, WS): BO 1 st, purl to end—1 st dec'd.

ROW 3 (RS): Knit.

ROW 4 (WS): Purl.

Rep the last 4 rows 5 (2, 0) times—92 (104, 114) sts; 25 (31, 38) sts for front, 52 (56, 58) sts for side, and 15 (17, 18) sts for back.

Shape Front Edge

All Sizes:

> **Note:** Bust shaping is complete; remove markers on next row.

Rows 135–148 (148, 148, 140, 144)

ROWS 1 AND 3 (RS): Knit.

ROW 2 (FRONT DEC, WS): BO 1 (1, 1, 2, 3) sts, purl to end—1 (1, 1, 2, 3) sts dec'd.

ROW 4 (WS): Purl.

Rep the last 4 rows 2 (2, 2, 0, 1) times, then work Rows 1 and 2 once more—88 (100, 110, 124, 134) sts.

Sizes 40 (44)" only:

Rows 141 (145)–148

ROWS 1 AND 3 (RS): Knit.

ROW 2 (WS): Purl.

ROW 4 (FRONT DEC, WS): BO 1 (2) sts, purl to end—1 (2) sts dec'd.

Rep the last 4 rows 1 (0) times—122 (132) sts.

Left Back

> **Note:** As you work the instructions below, work all rows in color A.

All Sizes:

ROW 149 (RS): K39 (44, 49, 54, 58), k2tog, k1, put next 4 (6, 6, 8, 10) sts on a st holder or waste yarn for underarm, put rem 42 (47, 52, 57, 61) sts on a separate st holder or waste yarn for the left front—41 (46, 51, 56, 60) sts rem for left back.

Shape Armhole

Rows 150–155 (157, 163, 169, 169)

Purl 1 WS row.

DEC ROW (RS): Knit to last 3 sts, k2tog, k1—1 st dec'd.

Rep the last 2 rows 2 (3, 6, 9, 9) times—38 (42, 44, 46, 50) sts rem.

Rows 156 (158, 164, 170, 170)–205 (205, 207, 207, 207)

Work 50 (48, 44, 38, 38) rows even in St st, ending after a RS row.

Shape Shoulder

Rows 206 (206, 208, 208, 208)–223 (225, 229, 229, 231)

ROW 1 (WS): P1, p2tog, purl to end—1 st dec'd.

ROW 2 (RS): Knit to last 3 sts, k2tog, k1—1 st dec'd.

Rep the last 2 rows 8 (9, 10, 10, 11) times—20 (22, 22, 24, 26) sts rem.

Sizes 29 (33, 40, 44)" only:

Row 224 (226, 230, 233)

NEXT ROW (WS): P1, p2tog, purl to end—19 (21, 23, 25) sts rem.

All Sizes:

Break yarn and put sts onto a st holder or waste yarn to use for the edging later.

Left Front

> **Note:** As you work the instructions below, work all rows in color A.

Return 42 (47, 52, 57, 61) held left front sts onto needle and join color A preparing to work a RS row.

Shape Armhole and Neck

Rows 149–156 (156, 164, 168, 168)

ROWS 1 AND 3 (ARMHOLE DEC, RS): K1, ssk, knit to end—1 st dec'd.

ROW 2 (WS): Purl.

ROW 4 (FRONT DEC, WS): BO 1 st, purl to end—1 st dec'd.

Rep the last 4 rows 1 (1, 3, 4, 4) times—36 (41, 40, 42, 46) sts rem.

Sizes 33 (40, 44)" only:

Row 157 (169, 169)

ROW 1 (ARMHOLE DEC, RS): K1, ssk, knit to end—40 (41, 45) sts rem.

Row 158 (170, 170)

ROW 2 (WS): Purl.

Sizes 29 (36)" only:

Rows 157 (165)–158 (166)

Work 2 rows even in St st, ending after a WS row.

All Sizes:

Rows 159 (159, 167, 171, 171)–214 (218, 222, 222, 230)

ROWS 1 AND 3 (RS): Knit.

ROW 2 (FRONT DEC, WS): BO 1 st, purl to end—1 st dec'd.

ROW 4 (WS): Purl.

Rep the last 4 rows 13 (14, 13, 12, 14) times—22 (25, 26, 28, 30) sts rem.

Rows 215 (217, 223, 223, 231)–224 (226, 229, 230, 232)

Work 10 (8, 7, 8, 2) rows even in St st.

BO all sts loosely.

Right Body

> **Note:** As you work the instructions below, beg Stripe Patt on Row 81. Work all other rows in color A.

With color A and cir, use a provisional method to CO 76 (93, 105, 121, 136) sts. Do not join; work back and forth in rows.

Shape Front

Rows 1–5 (5, 7, 7, 7)

Knit 1 RS row.

INC ROW (WS): Purl to end, use the backward loop method to CO 2 sts—2 sts inc'd.

Rep the last 2 rows 1 (1, 2, 2, 2) times, then knit 1 RS row—80 (97, 111, 127, 142) sts.

Sizes 29 (33)" only:
Rows 6–13

INC ROW (WS): Purl to end, CO 1 st—1 st inc'd.

Knit 1 RS row.

Rep the last 2 rows 3 times—84 (101) sts.

Shape Hip
All Sizes:
ROW 14 (14, 8, 8, 8) (WS): P15 (17, 18, 20, 22) for back, pm, p52 (56, 60, 64, 68) for side, pm, p17 (28, 33, 43, 52) to end for front, CO 1 (1, 2, 2, 2) sts—85 (102, 113, 129, 144) sts.

Rows 15 (15, 9, 9, 9)–56 (56, 68, 68, 74)

ROWS 1 AND 3 (RS): Knit.

ROWS 2, 4, AND 6 (FRONT INC, WS): Purl to end, CO 1—1 st inc'd.

ROW 5 (HIP DEC, RS): Knit to first m, sl m, ssk, knit to 2 st before next m, k2tog, sl m, knit to end—2 sts dec'd.

Rep the last 6 rows 6 (6, 9, 9, 10) times—92 (109, 123, 139, 155) sts; 15 (17, 18, 20, 22) sts for back, 38 (42, 40, 44, 46) sts for side, and 39 (50, 65, 75, 87) sts for front.

Rows 57 (57, 69, 69, 75)–80

ROWS 1 AND 3 (RS): Knit.

ROWS 2 AND 4 (WS): Purl.

ROW 5 (HIP DEC, RS): Knit to first m, sl m, ssk, knit to 2 st before next m, k2tog, sl m, knit to end—2 sts dec'd.

ROW 6 (FRONT INC, WS): Purl to end, CO 1—1 st inc'd.

Rep the last 6 rows 3 (3, 1, 1, 0) times—88 (105, 121, 137, 154) sts; 15 (17, 18, 20, 22) sts for back, 30 (34, 36, 40, 44) sts for side, and 43 (54, 67, 77, 88) sts for front.

Waist

> **Note:** *If you adjusted the length in the waist section on the left body, make an equal adjustment in this section, placing the "Tie-hole Row" at the center and ending after a WS row.*

ROWS 81–84: Work 4 rows even in St st, ending after a WS row.

TIE-HOLE ROW (RS): Knit to first m, sl m, k15 (17, 18, 20, 22), yo, k2tog, knit to end.

ROWS 86–90: Work 5 rows even in St st, ending after a WS row.

Place a removable m into the first and last st of the last row. You'll use the markers when you sew the back seam and apply the front edging.

Shape Bust
Rows 91–98 (106, 122, 126, 134)

ROW 1 (BUST INC, FRONT DEC, RS): BO 3 sts, knit to first m, sl m, M1, knit to next m, M1, sl m, knit to end—1 st dec'd.

ROWS 2 AND 4 (WS): Purl.

ROW 3 (RS): Knit.

Rep the last 4 rows 1 (3, 7, 8, 10) times—86 (101, 113, 128, 143) sts rem; 15 (17, 18, 20, 22) sts for back, 34 (42, 52, 58, 66) sts for side, and 37 (42, 43, 50, 55) sts for front.

Sizes 29 (33, 36, 40)" only:
Rows 99 (107, 123, 127)–110 (122, 130, 134)

ROW 1 (BUST INC, FRONT DEC, RS): BO 2 sts, knit to first m, sl m, M1, knit to next m, M1, sl m, knit to end.

ROWS 2 AND 4 (WS): Purl.

ROW 3 (RS): Knit.

Rep the last 4 rows 2 (3, 1, 1) times—86 (101, 113, 128) sts; 15 (17, 18, 20) sts for back, 40 (50, 56, 62) sts for side, and 31 (34, 39, 46) sts for front.

Sizes 29 (33, 36)" only:
Rows 111 (123, 131)–134

ROW 1 (BUST INC, FRONT DEC, RS): BO 1 sts, knit to first m, sl m, M1, knit to next m, M1, sl m, knit to end—1 st inc'd.

ROWS 2 AND 4 (WS): Purl.

ROW 3 (RS): Knit.

Rep the last 4 rows 5 (2, 0) times—92 (104, 114) sts; 15 (17, 18) sts for back, 52 (56, 58) sts for side, and 25 (31, 38) sts for front.

Shape Front Edge
All Sizes:

> **Note:** *Bust shaping is complete; remove markers on next row.*

Rows 135–148 (148, 148, 140, 144)

ROW 1 (FRONT DEC, RS): BO 1 (1, 1, 2, 3) sts, knit to end—1 (1, 1, 2, 3) sts dec'd.

ROWS 2 AND 4 (WS): Purl.

ROW 3 (RS): Knit.

Rep the last 4 rows 2 (2, 2, 0, 1) times, then work Rows 1 and 2 once more—88 (100, 110, 124, 134) sts.

Sizes 40 (44)" only:
Rows 141 (145)–148

ROW 1 (FRONT DEC, RS): BO 1 (2) sts, knit to end—1 (2) sts dec'd.

ROWS 2 AND 4 (WS): Purl.

ROW 3 (RS): Knit.

Rep the last 4 rows 1 (0) times—122 (132) sts.

Right Front

All Sizes:

> **Note:** *As you work the instructions below, beg Stripe Patt on Row 173.*

ROW 149 (RS): K39 (44, 49, 54, 58), k2tog, k1, put the next 4 (6, 6, 8, 10) sts on a st holder or waste yarn for underarm, put rem 42 (47, 52, 57, 61) sts on a separate holder for the right back—41 (46, 51, 56, 60) sts rem for right front.

Purl 1 WS row.

Shape Armhole and Neck
Rows 151–154 (158, 162, 170, 170)

ROW 1 (ARMHOLE AND NECK DEC, RS): BO 1, knit to last 3 sts, k2tog, k1—2 sts dec'd.

ROWS 2 AND 4 (WS): Purl.

ROW 3 (ARMHOLE DEC, RS): Knit to last 3 sts, k2tog, k1—1 st dec'd.

Rep the last 4 rows 0 (1, 2, 4, 4) times—38 (40, 42, 41, 45) sts rem.

Sizes 29 (36)" only:
Rows 155 (163)–158 (166)

NEXT ROW (ARMHOLE AND NECK DEC, RS): BO 1, knit to last 3 sts, k2tog, k1—36 (40) sts rem.

Work 3 rows even in St st, ending after a WS row.

All Sizes:
Rows 159 (159, 167, 171, 171)
214 (218, 222, 222, 230)

ROW 1 (FRONT DEC, RS): BO 1 st, knit to end—1 st dec'd.

ROWS 2 AND 4 (WS): Purl.

ROW 3 (RS): Knit.

Rep the last 4 rows 13 (14, 13, 12, 14) times—22 (25, 26, 28, 30) sts rem.

Work 10 (8, 7, 8, 2) rows even in St st.

224 (226, 229, 230, 232) rows worked to here.

BO all sts loosely.

Right Back

> **Note:** *As you work the instructions below, beg Stripe Patt on Row 173.*

Return 42 (47, 52, 57, 61) held right back sts onto needle and join color A preparing to work a RS row.

Shape Armhole
Rows 149–156 (158, 164, 170, 170)

ROW 1 (RS): K1, ssk, knit to end—41 (46, 51, 56, 60) sts rem.

ROW 2 (WS): Purl.

Rep the last 2 rows 3 (4, 7, 10, 10) times—38 (42, 44, 46, 50) sts rem.

Rows 157 (159, 165, 171, 171)–205 (205, 207, 207, 207)

Work 49 (47, 43, 37, 37) rows even in St st, ending after a RS row.

Shape Shoulder
Rows 206 (206, 208, 208, 208)–223 (225, 229, 229, 231)

ROW 1 (WS): Purl to last 3 sts, ssp, p1—1 st dec'd.

ROW 2 (RS): K1, ssk, knit to end—1 st dec'd.

Rep the last 2 rows 8 (9, 10, 10, 11) times—20 (22, 22, 24, 26) sts rem.

ROW 224 (226, 230, 232) (WS): Purl to last 3 sts, ssp, p1—19 (21, 23, 25) sts rem.

All Sizes:

Break yarn and put sts onto a st holder or waste yarn to use for the edging later.

Seaming

Block pieces to measurements.

Using a yarn needle threaded with color A, sew the long straight edges of the right and left body pieces together with the mattress stitch (see Techniques), matching the markers in the center back. Sew the BO edge of the front shoulder to the slanted edge of the back shoulder. Remove the m at the center back when finished.

Sleeve

> *Note: The sleeves are worked from the top down. Beg by picking up sts around the armhole, work short-rows to form the sleeve cap, and then cont down the sleeve working circularly. Working from the top down allows for easy length and circumference adjustment, so try on the sleeve periodically to test the fit. Because the front of the armhole is longer than the back, the shoulder seam is not exactly at the top of the shoulder. Be careful to pick up sts evenly.*

Divide 4 (6, 6, 8, 10) held sts from one underarm evenly onto 2 dpn. Beg at the center of underarm sts, with RS facing, color A and dpn, k2 (3, 3, 4, 5) held sts, pick up and knit 62 (68, 72, 78, 80) sts evenly around

the armhole, then knit the rem 2 (3, 3, 4, 5) held underarm sts—66 (74, 78, 86, 90) sts. Pm for beg of rnd.

Shape Sleeve Cap with Short-Rows (see Techniques) as foll:

SHORT-ROW 1 (RS): K44 (50, 52, 58, 60), w&t; p22 (26, 26, 30, 30), w&t—21 (23, 25, 27, 29) sts rem unwrapped at each end of row.

SHORT-ROW 2 (RS): Knit to wrapped st from the previous row, knit that st leaving the wrap intact, w&t; purl to the wrapped st from the previous row, purl that st leaving the wrap intact, w&t.

Rep the last short-row 18 (19, 21, 22, 23) times—2 (3, 3, 4, 5) sts rem unwrapped at each end of row.

NEXT ROW (RS): Knit to wrapped st from previous row, knit that st leaving the wrap intact, knit to end.

Shape Sleeve

> *Note: Beg keeping track of row numbers for Stripe Patt. As you work the next section, begin the stripe pattern on Rnd 2 for the right sleeve, and on Rnd 47 for the left sleeve. Work all other rows with color A. The sleeve is meant to fit snugly through the forearm. This close fit helps support the weight of the sleeves so the very open front won't gape, so try on the sleeve often to be sure it fits your body correctly. If sleeves are too tight, adjust spacing of dec rnds to be farther apart, or if too loose, work dec rnds closer together.*

Knit 8 (6, 6, 5, 5) rnds.

DEC RND: Ssk, knit to last 2 sts, k2tog—2 sts dec'd.

Rep the last 9 (7, 7, 6, 6) rnds 10 (13, 13, 15, 15) times—44 (46, 50, 54, 58) sts rem.

Work even until the sleeve meas 12½" (31.5 cm) from pick-up rnd.

Edging

Change to color B and knit 1 rnd.

Purl 6 rnds.

BO all sts loosely kwise, leaving a very long tail when you break yarn.

Turn the sleeve inside out, thread the long tail onto a yarn needle. Turn the edging toward the WS, and sew the hem into place, attaching the BO edge to the purl bumps on the first row of color B stripe.

Work second sleeve the same as the first.

Finishing

Block piece to measurements.

A contrasting border is added to the cardigan in two parts. The first part is the lower edge, beg at the waist and working down the curved edge, across the lower cast-on edge, then back up the other curved edge to the waist level of the other side. The second part is worked from the waist up to the shoulders, around the back of the neck, and then down to the waist level of the other side. For the best-looking results, pick up all the stitches in a nice smooth line about ¼"–½" (6–13 mm) away from the edge of the cardigan, being especially careful to keep the line smooth along the curved edges.

Upper Edging

With RS facing, cir and color B, beg at waist level of the right front, pick up and knit 3 sts from the selvedge edge of the lower edging, 105 (120, 130, 140, 140) sts along the neck edge to the shoulder seam, return 38 (42, 44, 46, 50) held neck sts to empty end of needle and knit across, pick up and knit 105 (120, 130, 140, 140) sts along the neck edge to the lower edging on the left front, then 3 sts along the selvedge edge of the lower edging—254 (288, 310, 332, 336) sts.

Cont working the same as for lower edging.

I-Cord Tie

With color B and a dpn, CO 6 sts.

Work i-cord (see Techniques) over the 6 sts until the piece meas about 32 (36, 40, 44, 48)" (81.5 [91.5, 101.5, 112, 122] cm) from beg.

Break yarn, leaving a 6" (15 cm) tail.

Thread the tail onto a yarn needle and run the needle through the 6 sts, pulling it tight to cinch them together. Secure the end.

Attach the CO edge of the i-cord to the selvedge edge of the upper edging.

Make a second i-cord tie attaching it to the other selvedge edge of the upper edging.

Weave in ends.

Lower Edging

With RS facing, cir and color B, beg at the removable m on the left front, pick up and knit 7 sts from the straight part at the waist (adjust this number if you adjusted the length of the cardigan in the waist section), 64 (64, 67, 67, 68) sts along the curved edge to the lower cast-on edge, carefully remove waste yarn from provisional CO sts of left body and place 76 (99, 105, 121, 136) sts on empty end of needle, then knit across, carefully remove waste yarn from provisional CO sts of right body and place 76 (99, 105, 121, 136) sts on empty end of needle, then knit across, pick up and knit 64 (64, 67, 67, 68) sts along the curved edge to the flat edge of the right front piece, then 7 sts along the waist section to the other removable marker (adjust this number if you adjusted the length of the cardigan in the waist section)—294 (328, 358, 390, 422) sts.

Work in Rev St st (purl on RS, knit on WS) for 6 rows, ending after a RS row.

BO all sts pwise.

Thread a long length of color B onto a yarn needle. With the WS facing, turn the edging toward the WS, and sew the BO edge of edging to the purl bumps on the first rnd of the contrasting stripe with a whipstitch or horizontal mattress stitch (recommended). Close the ends of the edging neatly, hiding any loose ends inside of the border.

liwi top

THIS SLEEVELESS TOP FEATURES asymmetrical mesh panels, and a cute cutout effect on the top of the shoulders. The cutout effect occurs without any special shaping, so you can optionally sew the opening closed for a more modest look. The armhole and shoulder cutouts have a garter stitch edging, and the neck edge is finished with a stockinette rolled hem.

FINISHED SIZE
About 27 (30¾, 34¾, 38½, 42¼)" (68.5 [78, 88.5, 98, 107.5] cm) bust circumference

Top shown measures 30¾" (78 cm).

YARN
DK weight (#3 Light)

Shown here: Rowan Baby Merino Silk DK (66% superwash wool, 34% silk; 147 yd [135 m]/50 g): 687 Strawberry, 4 (5, 5, 6, 7) skeins.

NEEDLES
Size U.S. 5 (3.75 mm): 24" (60 cm) circular (cir).

Size U.S. 6 (4 mm): 24" (60 cm) cir.

Adjust needle size if necessary to obtain the correct gauge.

NOTIONS
Stitch markers (m)

Stitch holders or waste yarn

Yarn needle

Four ⅜" (1 cm) decorative buttons (optional)

Sewing needle and matching thread for buttons

GAUGE
21 sts and 31 rnds = 4" (10 cm) in St st.

18 sts and 29 rows = 4" (10 cm) in Divided Mesh Patt.

Stitch Guide
Divided Mesh Pattern

*(**Note:** With RS facing, an odd number of sts is needed to the right of a marker, and an even number of sts is needed to the left.)*

(also, see chart)

ROWS 1 AND 3 (WS): K3, purl to last 3 sts, k3.

ROW 2 (RS): K4, [k2tog, yo] to 1 st before m, k1, sl m, k2, [yo, ssk] to last 4 sts, k4.

ROW 4 (RS): K3, [k2tog, yo] to m, sl m, k1, [yo, ssk] to last 3 sts, k3.

Rep Rows 1–4 for patt.

Notes

Liwi is worked from the bottom up circularly to the underarm, then the stitches are divided and front and back are worked flat to form the armholes. During finishing, the front and back are sewn together at two points on each shoulder, then decorative buttons are sewn on top of these points.

Body
Lower Edging

With smaller cir, CO 162 (182, 202, 222, 242) sts. Place marker (pm) and join to work in the rnd, being careful not to twist sts.

NEXT 6 RNDS: *K1, p1; rep from *.

Change to larger cir and work in St st (knit all sts, every rnd) for 1" (2.5 cm).

Shape Sides

Set-up Rnd: K20 (23, 25, 28, 30), pm, k41 (45, 51, 55, 61), pm, k40 (46, 50, 56, 60), pm, k41 (45, 51, 55, 61), pm, k20 (23, 25, 28, 30) to end.

DEC RND: *Knit to 2 sts before m, k2tog, knit to next m, sl m, ssk; rep from * once more, knit to end—4 sts dec'd.

Knit 9 rnds.

Rep the last 10 rnds 4 times—142 (162, 182, 202, 222) sts rem.

> **Note:** Side shaping is complete; discard the markers as you work the next row.

Work even in St st until piece meas 15½" (39.5 cm) from CO.

PM FOR MESH AND UNDERARMS: K28 (32, 37, 42, 47), pm for front mesh, k39 (45, 49, 53, 57), pm for underarm, k32 (36, 42, 48, 54), pm for back mesh, k42 (48, 52, 56, 60) to last 1 (1, 2, 3, 4) sts, place a new beg of rnd m (discard the old beg of rnd m as you work the next row).

RND 1: P5 (5, 7, 9, 11), knit to second m, sl m, p8 (8, 10, 12, 14), knit to last 3 sts, p3.

RND 2: Knit.

Rep the last 2 rnds, then rep Rnd 1 once more.

Front
Divide Back and Front
Sizes 27 (34¾, 42¼)" only:

BO 2 (4, 8) sts, knit until 3 sts are on right needle, [k2tog, yo] 12 (16, 20) times to first m, sl m, k1, [yo, ssk] 19 (24, 28) times to next m, remove m, k3, put rem 71 (91, 111) sts on a st holder or waste yarn for back, keeping the m in place—69 (87, 103) sts rem for front. Cont working back and forth on front sts only.

DIVIDED MESH CHART

				knit on RS, purl on WS			yo
				purl on RS, knit on WS			ssk
				stitch marker			pattern repeat
				k2tog			

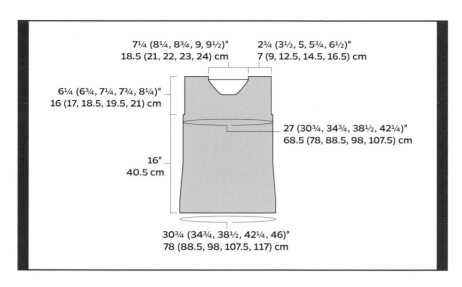

7¼ (8¼, 8¾, 9, 9½)"
18.5 (21, 22, 23, 24) cm

2¾ (3½, 5, 5¾, 6½)"
7 (9, 12.5, 14.5, 16.5) cm

6¼ (6¾, 7¼, 7¾, 8¼)"
16 (17, 18.5, 19.5, 21) cm

27 (30¾, 34¾, 38½, 42¼)"
68.5 (78, 88.5, 98, 107.5) cm

16"
40.5 cm

30¾ (34¾, 38½, 42¼, 46)"
78 (88.5, 98, 107.5, 117) cm

Sizes 30¾ (38½)" only:

BO 2 (6) sts, knit until 4 sts are on the right needle, [k2tog, yo] 13 (17) times to 1 st before m, k1, sl m, k2, [yo, ssk] 21 (25) times to 1 st before next m, k1, remove m, k3, put rem 81 (101) sts on a st holder or waste yarn for back, keeping the m in place—79 (95) sts rem for front. Cont working back and forth on front sts only.

NEXT ROW (WS): K3, purl to last 3 sts, k3.

NEXT ROW (RS): K3, [k2tog, yo] to first m, sl m, k1, [yo, ssk] to last 3 sts, k3.

All Sizes:

Work Rows 1–4 of Divided Mesh Patt 5 (5, 6, 6, 7) times, then work Rows 1–3 again.

Divide for Neck

NEXT ROW (RS): K3, [k2tog, yo] 11 (13, 15, 17, 19) times to 2 sts before m, k2tog, remove m, put the next 15 (17, 17, 17, 17) sts onto a st holder or waste yarn, put the rem 27 (31, 35, 39, 43) sts on a separate holder for the right front—26 (30, 34, 38, 42) sts rem for left front. Cont working back and forth on left front sts only.

Left Front
Shape Neck

ROWS 1 AND 3 (WS): Purl to last 3 sts, k3.

ROW 2 (RS): K4, [k2tog, yo] to last 2 sts, k2tog—1 st dec'd.

ROW 4 (RS): K3, [k2tog, yo] to last 2 sts, k2tog—1 st dec'd.

Rep the last 4 rows 3 (4, 4, 5, 5) times—18 (20, 24, 26, 30) sts rem.

Sizes 27 (34¾, 42¼)" only:

Rep Rows 1 and 2 of neck shaping once more—17 (23, 29) sts rem.

Button Tab

All Sizes:

Work even in Gtr st (knit all sts, every row) for 6 rows.

BO loosely.

Right Front

Return the 27 (31, 35, 39, 43) held right front sts onto larger cir and join yarn preparing to work a RS row.

Shape Neck

NEXT ROW: Ssk, [yo, ssk] 11 (13, 14, 17, 19) times to last 3 sts, k3—26 (30, 34, 38, 42) rem.

ROWS 1 AND 3 (WS): K3, purl to end.

ROW 2 (RS): Ssk, [yo, ssk] to last 4 sts, k4—1 st dec'd.

ROW 4 (RS): Ssk, [yo, ssk] to last 3 sts, k3—1 st dec'd.

Rep the last 4 rows 3 (4, 4, 5, 5) times—18 (20, 24, 26, 30) sts rem.

Sizes 27 (34¾, 42¼)" only:

Rep Rows 1 and 2 of neck shaping once more—17 (23, 29) sts rem.

Button Tab

All Sizes:

Work even in Gtr st for 6 rows.

BO loosely.

Back

Return the 71 (81, 91, 101, 111) held back sts onto larger cir and join yarn preparing to work a RS row.

SET-UP ROW (RS): BO 2 (2, 4, 6, 8) sts, knit until 3 sts are on right needle, [k2tog, yo] 12 (14, 16, 18, 20) times to m, sl m, k1, [yo, ssk] 19 (22, 24, 26, 28) times to last 3 sts, k3—69 (79, 87, 95, 103) sts rem.

Work Rows 1–4 of Divided Mesh Patt 10 (11, 12, 13, 14) times, then work Rows 1 and 2 again.

Right Button Tab

Divide for Button Tabs (WS): K17 (20, 23, 26, 29), put the next 35 (39, 41, 43, 45) sts on a st holder or waste yarn for the back neck, put rem 17 (20, 23, 26, 29) sts on a st holder or waste yarn for the left button tab—17 (20, 23, 26, 29) sts rem.

Work in Gtr st for 6 rows.

BO loosely.

Creative Accidents

My favorite part of designing is creating my initial sketch. I love to draw, so I rely heavily on this first phase of my process to work out many of the finer details and construction techniques I plan to use. I really trust my sketches and try to execute them as closely as possible when I'm creating my patterns, but I also think it's important to keep an open mind. Some of my best work has been born out of creative accidents.

In the process of creating the sample for Liwi, I was lucky enough to have one of those marvelous creative accidents. As I finished knitting the sample, I could hardly wait to pin the shoulders into place so I could try it on for the first time. This is always an exciting moment for a knitter. As I was inspecting my handiwork in the mirror, twisting my shoulders this way and that to peek at the back, one of the pins popped off and my pointy freckled shoulder popped right through the hole. I thought, hey that's cool, too!

In my initial sketch, I intended to close the shoulders and attach a row of buttons. I tried it both ways, with and without the cutout effect. They both looked cute, but I decided that my creative accident gave the design just a bit of fun edgy flair. I encourage you to try it both ways, too. Who knows, maybe you'll have a happy creative accident of your own!

Left Button Tab

Return the 17 (20, 23, 26, 29) left button tab sts to larger cir and join yarn preparing to work a WS row.

Work in Gtr st for 6 rows.

BO loosely.

Finishing

Block piece to measurements.

Front Neck Edging

With RS of front facing and larger cir, beg at neck edge of left front button tab, pick up and knit 4 sts along the side of the button tab, 18 (20, 22, 24, 26) sts along the angled edge of neck, place the 15 (17, 17, 17, 17) held front neck sts onto empty end of needle and knit across, pick up and knit 18 (20, 22, 24, 26) sts along the angled edge neck, then 4 sts along the side of the button tab—59 (65, 69, 73, 77) sts.

Work 3 rows in St st.

BO very loosely, holding a larger needle in your right hand if necessary.

Back Neck Edging

With RS back facing and larger cir, beg at neck edge of right back button tab, pick up and knit 4 sts along the side of the button tab, place the 35 (39, 41, 43, 45) held back neck sts onto empty end of needle and knit across, pick up and knit 4 sts along the side of the button tab—43 (47, 49, 51, 53) sts.

Work 3 rows in St st

BO very loosely, holding a larger needle in your right hand if necessary.

Seam Shoulders

Turn the garment WS out. With WS facing, layer the back button tabs over the front button tabs (so on the RS the front tabs are on the top). With small neat sts, sew the tabs together along the edges of the armhole and the neck edges where the rolled hem meets the button tab.

Turn the garment RS out. Position 2 buttons on each shoulder about ½" (1.3 cm) from the ends of the button tabs. With sewing thread and needle, attach the buttons sewing through both layers.

Weave in loose ends.

danae mittens

THE EYE-CATCHING LOOPING diamond patterns on these mittens have a rhythm to them that will keep you wanting to knit just one more round. The Fair Isle color work creates a double layer of yarn that will keep your hands extra warm on cold windy days. Details like fully patterned thumb gussets and shaping integrated into the color work make these mittens interesting to knit and a pleasure to show off and wear.

FINISHED SIZE

7½" (19 cm) hand circumference and 9¾" (25 cm) long.

YARN

Fingering Weight (#1 Super Fine)

Shown here: Cascade 220 Fingering (100% Peruvian highland wool, 273 yd [250 m]/50 g): #7824 Jack o' Lantern (A) and #9592 Sage (B), 1 skein each.

NEEDLES

Size U.S. 1 (2.25 mm): set of 4 or 5 double-pointed (dpn)

Adjust needle size if necessary to obtain the correct gauge.

NOTIONS

Stitch markers (m)

Stitch holders or waste yarn

Yarn needle

GAUGE

39 sts and 44 rnds = 4" (10 cm) in Mitten Chart.

Notes

Each mitten is worked circularly from the cuff to the fingertips. The cuff of the mitten is worked without shaping to the base of the thumb gusset. Stitches for the thumb are gradually added through the Thumb Gusset section, then divided out and put on a holder at the thumb level. The top part of the mitten is worked without shaping to the fingertips, where the tip is tapered to a blunt point. The thumb is worked from a separate chart.

Make-One Increase (M1): *For the best-looking result when working this increase (see Techniques), make a backward loop on your right thumb and transfer it to your right needle as if to cast on a stitch.*

Cuff

With color A, CO 66 sts. Divide sts evenly over 3 or 4 dpn. Place marker (pm) for beg of rnd and join to work in the rnd, being careful not to twist sts.

NEXT RND: Purl.

NEXT RND: Change to color B and knit.

NEXT RND: Purl.

NEXT RND: Change to color A and knit.

NEXT RND: *P11, M1; rep from *—72 sts.

Work Rnds 1–20 of Mitten Chart.

Thumb Gusset

Work Rnds 21–53 of Mitten Chart—94 sts.

DIVIDE FOR THUMB: Put the next 25 sts onto a st holder or waste yarn, use the backward loop method (see Techniques) to CO 3 sts as indicated at beg of Rnd 54 of Mitten Chart, work to end of rnd—72 sts rem.

Top of Mitten

Work Rnds 55–91 of Mitten Chart.

RND 92: Work from the chart to the last st in the row, remove the beg of rnd m, k1 with color A, replace m.

Work Rnds 93–103 of Mitten Chart—12 sts rem.

Break yarn for both colors leaving a tail about 12" (30.5 cm) long. Thread both tails onto a yarn needle. Run the needle through the rem sts on the needle 2 times to cinch the top of the mitten closed. Secure the ends to the WS so the mitten will stay closed at the top.

Thumb

Return 25 held thumb sts onto 3 dpns. With a fourth dpn beg working Row 1 of the Thumb Chart by picking up the first stitch from the color B stripe that runs up the side of the mitten, cont by picking up the next 2 sts with color A along the edge of the gap, work to end of held sts, then pick up and knit the last 2 sts with color A along the edge of the gap—30 sts.

Work Rows 2–22 of Thumb Chart.

Break yarn for both colors leaving tail about 12" (30.5 cm) long. Thread both tails onto a yarn needle. Run the needle through the rem sts on the needle 2 times to cinch the top of the thumb closed. Secure the ends to the WS so the thumb will stay closed at the top.

Make second mitten the same as the first.

Finishing

Weave in the loose ends. Wet-block the mittens so the sts will even out and lie flat.

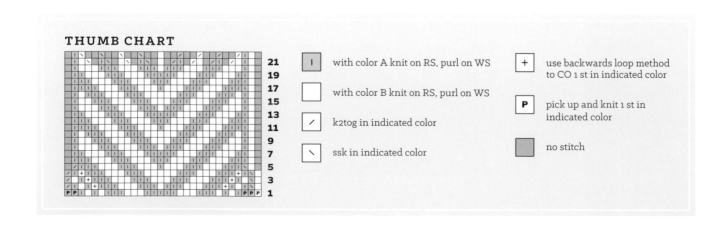

THUMB CHART

21
19
17
15
13
11
9
7
5
3
1

I	with color A knit on RS, purl on WS
	with color B knit on RS, purl on WS
/	k2tog in indicated color
\	ssk in indicated color
+	use backwards loop method to CO 1 st in indicated color
P	pick up and knit 1 st in indicated color
	no stitch

MITTEN CHART

I with color A knit on RS, purl on WS	**** ssk in indicated color	**P** pick up and knit 1 st in indicated color
☐ with color B knit on RS, purl on WS	**+** use backwards loop method to CO 1 st in indicated color	☐ no stitch
/ k2tog in indicated color	— put sts onto a st holder or waste yarn	☐ pattern repeat

trilogy
cardigan

THIS FLOWING DRAPED CARDIGAN has a strong graphic look and comes together in a very entertaining way. The unusual construction gives the illusion of intarsia blocks, but with much cleaner diagonal lines. The open draped front can be worn in a variety of ways by buttoning the corners to hidden buttons behind the shoulder inside the cardigan.

FINISHED SIZE

About 12½ (14, 14½, 15½, 17)" (31.5 [35.5, 37, 39.5, 43] cm) across the upper back shoulders. Select a size that most closely matches your shoulder width, but the sizes are also meant to correspond with size 32 (36, 40, 44, 48)" bust circumference.

Cardigan shown measures 14" (35.5 cm).

YARN

Sport (#2 Fine)

Shown here: Blue Sky Alpacas Sport (100% alpaca; 110 yd [100 m]/50 g): #518 Scarlet (A), 7 (7, 7, 8, 8) skeins; #516 Petal Pink (B), 6 (6, 6, 7, 7) skeins.

NEEDLES

Cardigan and Sleeves: Size U.S. 7 (4.5 mm): straight.

Ribbing: Size U.S. 7 (4.5 mm): 32" (81.5 cm) circular (cir).

Adjust needle size if necessary to obtain the correct gauge.

NOTIONS

Stitch markers (m)

Stitch holders or waste yarn

Smooth waste yarn for provisional cast-on

Yarn needle

Size F/5 (3.25 mm) crochet hook (for button loops)

Two ½" (1.3 cm) buttons

Sewing needle (for buttons)

Matching thread (for buttons)

GAUGE

19 sts and 27 rows = 4" (10 cm) in St st.

Stitch Guide

1 × 1 Rib (multiple of 2 sts):

ROW 1: *K1, p1; rep from *.

Rep Row 1 for patt.

Notes

The angular blocks of color are worked into 3 long strips that are shaped by simple increases and decreases. Sleeve caps are worked into the middle strip, then the sleeves are worked from the top down from a provisional cast-on. At the end, the 3 long strips are sewn together. The edging is picked up from each edge and worked in 4 parts. Hidden crocheted button loops are attached to the edging, and buttons are attached in 2 places inside the cardigan.

Because this design uses both stockinette and reverse stockinette, it can be difficult to quickly see if you're working on the RS or the WS. To make this easier, tie a little bow on the RS with a contrasting piece of yarn.

Top Strip

> **Note:** *The top strip is worked in 2 pieces that are joined together when working the center panel.*

Left Base Triangle

CO 6 with color A.

SET-UP ROW (RS): [Kfb] twice, k1, pm, [kfb] twice, k1—10 sts.

ROW 1 (WS): Purl to 2 sts before m, pfb, p1, sl m, pfb, purl to end—2 sts inc'd.

ROW 2 (RS): Kfb, knit to 2 st before m, kfb, k1, sl m, kfb, knit to last 2 sts, kfb, k1—4 sts inc'd.

Rep the last 2 rows 15 times, then work Row 1 again—108 sts; 54 sts each side of m.

Size 12½" only:

Break yarn for color A. Holding the work with the RS facing, put 54 sts before the m onto a st holder or waste yarn for the center panel—54 sts rem.

Sizes 14 (14½, 15½, 17)" only:

NEXT ROW (RS): Kfb, knit to 2 sts before m, k2tog, remove m, put rem 54 sts onto a st holder or waste yarn for left extension—54 sts rem.

ROW 1 (WS): Purl.

ROW 2 (RS): Kfb, knit to last 2 sts, k2tog.

Rep the last 2 rows 0 (1, 2, 4) times, then work Row 1 once more—54 sts.

Break yarn for color A and put rem 54 sts onto a second st holder or waste yarn for the center panel.

Return the 54 held sts from the first st holder onto needle preparing to work a RS row.

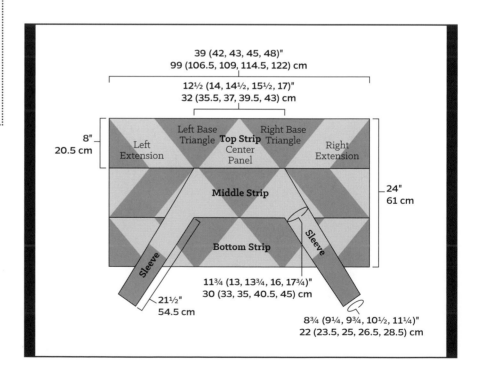

Left Extension

All Sizes:

NEXT ROW (RS): Join color B, ssk, knit to last st, kfb.

ROW 1 (WS): Knit

ROW 2 (RS): P2tog, purl to last st, pfb.

Rep the last 2 rows 15 (17, 18, 19, 21) times, then work Row 1 once more—54 sts; 34 (38, 40, 42, 46) rows worked in color B.

Break yarn for color B and join color A.

NEXT ROW (RS): Ssk, knit to last st, kfb.

ROW 1 (WS): P2tog, purl to end—1 st dec'd

ROW 2 (RS): Ssk, knit to last 2 sts, k2tog—2 sts dec'd.

Rep the last 2 rows 16 times—3 sts rem.

LAST ROW (WS): K3tog—1 st rem.

Break yarn, pull end through the last st to fasten off.

Right Base Triangle

CO 6 with color A.

SET-UP ROW (RS): [Kfb] twice, k1, pm, [kfb] twice, k1—10 sts.

ROW 1 (WS): Purl to 2 sts before m, pfb, p1, sl m, pfb, purl to end—2 sts inc'd.

ROW 2 (RS): Kfb, knit to 2 sts before m, kfb, k1, sl m, kfb, knit to last 2 sts, kfb, k1—4 sts inc'd.

Rep the last 2 rows 15 times, then work Row 1 again—108 sts; 54 sts each side of m.

Size 12½" only:

NEXT ROW (RS): Break yarn for color A and join color B, kfb, knit to 2 sts before m, k2tog, put rem 54 sts onto a st holder or waste yarn for the center panel—54 sts rem.

Sizes 14 (14½, 15½, 17)" only:

NEXT ROW (RS): Knit to m, put the 54 sts before m that you just worked onto a st holder or waste yarn for right extension, remove the m, ssk, knit to last st, kfb—54 sts rem.

ROW 1 (WS): Purl.

ROW 2 (RS): Ssk, knit to last st, kfb.

Rep the last 2 rows 0 (1, 2, 4) times, then work Row 1 once more—54 sts.

Break yarn for color A and put rem 54 sts onto a second st holder or waste yarn for the center panel.

NEXT ROW (RS): Return the 54 held sts from the first holder onto needle preparing to work a RS row. Join color B, kfb, knit to last 2 sts, k2tog.

Right Extension

All Sizes:

ROW 1 (WS): Knit.

ROW 2 (RS): Pfb, purl to last 2 sts, ssp.

Rep the last 2 rows 15 (17, 18, 19, 21) times, then work Row 1 once more—54 sts; 34 (38, 40, 42, 46) rows worked in color B.

Break yarn for color B and join color A.

NEXT ROW (RS): Kfb, knit to last 2 sts, k2tog.

ROW 1 (WS): Purl to last 2 sts, ssp—1 st dec'd.

ROW 2 (RS): Ssk, knit to last 2 sts, k2tog—2 sts dec'd.

Rep the last 2 rows 16 times—3 sts rem.

LAST ROW (WS): Sk2p (see Techniques)—1 st rem.

Break yarn, pull end through the last st to fasten off.

Center Panel

Return the 54 held right base triangle sts onto needle and join color B preparing to work a RS row; ssk, knit to last 2 sts, k2tog, return the 54 held left base triangle sts onto empty needle preparing to work a RS row; pm, ssk, knit to last 2 sts, k2tog—104 sts; 52 sts each side of m.

ROW 1 (WS): Knit to 2 sts before m, k2tog, sl m, ssk, knit to end—2 sts dec'd.

ROW 2 (RS): P2tog, purl to 2 sts before m, ssp, sl m, p2tog, purl to last 2 sts, ssp—4 sts dec'd.

Rep the last 2 rows 15 times—8 sts rem.

LAST ROW (WS): Ssk, k2tog, sl m, ssk, k2tog—4 sts rem.

Break yarn leaving an 8" (20.5 cm) tail and thread end onto a yarn needle. Run the needle through the rem sts twice to cinch them together. Secure end.

Bottom Strip

Work the same as the top strip.

Middle Strip

> **Note:** This strip is constructed similarly to the top and bottom strips, but with the addition of a sleeve cap that is worked into each of the base triangles. Sts are CO using a provisional method, which will be used later to knit the sleeves.

Left Sleeve Cap

With color B, use a provisional method (see Techniques) to CO 56 (62, 70, 76, 84).

SET-UP ROW (RS): Pfb, p2, pm, purl to last 3 sts, pm, p1, pfb, p1—58 (64, 72, 78, 86) sts.

Sizes 12½ (14, 14½)" only:

ROW 1 (WS): Knit.

ROW 2 (RS): Pfb, purl to 2 sts before m, pfb, p1, sl m, purl to the next m, sl m, pfb, purl to last 2 sts, pfb, p1—4 sts inc'd.

Rep the last 2 rows 8 (5, 1) times—94 (88, 80) sts; 22 (16, 8) sts between the edges and m on each side. Remove markers as you work next row.

All Sizes:

ROW 1 (WS): Knit.

ROW 2 (RS): Pfb, purl to last 2 sts, pfb, p1—2 sts inc'd.

Rep the last 2 rows 6 (9, 13, 14, 10) times—108 sts.

Sizes 15½ (17)" only:

ROW 1 (WS): Knit.

ROW 2 (RS): Pfb, purl to m, sl m, p2tog, purl to 2 sts before next m, ssp, sl m, purl to last 2 sts, pfb, p1.

Rep the last 2 rows 0 (4) times—108 sts.

Remove markers as you work next row.

All Sizes:

NEXT ROW (WS): K54, pm, k54 to end.

Size 12½" only:

Break yarn for color B. Holding the work with the RS facing, put 54 sts before the m onto a st holder or waste yarn for the center panel (note that the RS is reverse stockinette)—54 sts rem.

Sizes 14 (14½, 15½, 17)" only:

NEXT ROW (RS): Pfb, purl to 2 sts before m, ssp, remove m, put rem 54 sts onto a st holder or waste yarn for left extension—54 sts rem.

ROW 1 (WS): Knit.

ROW 2 (RS): Pfb, purl to last 2 sts, ssp.

Rep the last 2 rows 0 (1, 2, 4) times, then work Row 1 once more—54 sts.

Break yarn for color B and put rem 54 sts on second holder or waste yarn for the center panel.

Return the 54 held sts from the first holder onto needle preparing to work a RS row (note that the RS is reverse stockinette for color B).

Left Extension

All Sizes:

NEXT ROW (RS): Join color A, ssk, knit to last st, kfb.

ROW 1 (WS): Purl.

ROW 2 (RS): Ssk, knit to last st, kfb.

Rep the last 2 rows 15 (17, 18, 19, 21) times, then work Row 1 once more—54 sts; 34 (38, 40, 42, 46) rows worked in color A.

Break yarn for color A and join color B.

NEXT ROW (RS): Ssk, knit to last st, kfb.

ROW 1 (WS): Ssk, knit to end—1 st dec'd.

ROW 2 (RS): P2tog, purl to last 2 sts, ssp—2 sts dec'd.

Rep the last 2 rows 16 times—3 sts rem.

LAST ROW (WS): K3tog—1 st rem.

Break yarn, pull end through the last st to fasten off.

Right Sleeve Cap

With color B, use a provisional method (see Techniques) to CO 56 (62, 70, 76, 84).

SET-UP ROW (RS): Pfb, p2, pm, purl to last 3 sts, pm, p1, pfb, p1—58 (64, 72, 78, 86) sts.

Sizes 12½ (14, 14½)" only:

ROW 1 (WS): Knit.

ROW 2 (RS): Pfb, purl to 2 sts before m, pfb, p1, sl m, purl to the next m, sl m, pfb, purl to last 2 sts, pfb, p1—4 sts inc'd.

Rep the last 2 rows 8 (5, 1) times—94 (88, 80) sts; 22 (16, 8) sts between the edges and m on each side. Remove markers as you work next row.

All Sizes:

ROW 1 (WS): Knit.

ROW 2 (RS): Pfb, purl to last 2 sts, pfb, p1—2 sts inc'd.

Rep the last 2 rows 6 (9, 13, 14, 10) times—108 sts.

Sizes 15½ (17)" only:

ROW 1 (WS): Knit.

ROW 2 (RS): Pfb, purl to m, sl m, p2tog, purl to 2 sts before next m, ssp, sl m, purl to last 2 sts, pfb, p1.

Rep the last 2 rows 0 (4) times—108 sts.

Remove markers as you work next row.

All Sizes:

NEXT ROW (WS): K54, pm, k54 to end.

Size 12½" only:

Break yarn for color B and join color A, kfb, knit to 2 sts before m, k2tog, remove m, put rem 54 sts onto a st holder or waste yarn for the center panel—54 sts rem.

Sizes 14 (14½, 15½, 17)" only:

Purl to m, put the 54 sts before the m you just worked onto a st holder or waste yarn for right extension, remove m, p2tog, purl to last st, pfb—54 sts rem.

ROW 1 (WS): Knit.

ROW 2 (RS): P2tog, purl to last st, pfb.

Rep the last 2 rows 0 (1, 2, 4) times, then work Row 1 once more—54 sts.

Break yarn for color B and put rem 54 sts onto a second st holder or waste yarn for center panel.

NEXT ROW (RS): Return the 54 held sts from the first holder onto needle preparing to work a RS row (note that the RS is reverse stockinette for color B). Join color A, kfb, knit to last 2 sts, k2tog.

Right Extension

All Sizes:

ROW 1 (WS): Purl.

ROW 2 (RS): Kfb, knit to last 2 sts, k2tog.

Rep the last 2 rows 15 (17, 18, 19, 21) times, then work Row 1 once more— 54 sts; 34 (38, 40, 42, 46) rows worked in color A.

Break yarn for color A and join color B.

NEXT ROW (RS): Kfb, knit to last 2 sts, k2tog.

ROW 1 (WS): Knit to last 2 sts, k2tog— 1 st dec'd.

ROW 2 (RS): P2tog, purl to last 2 sts, ssp—2 sts dec'd.

Rep the last 2 rows 16 times—3 sts rem.

LAST ROW (WS): Sk2p—1 st rem.

Break yarn, pull end through the last st to fasten off.

Center Panel

Return the 54 held right sleeve cap sts onto needle and join color A preparing to work a RS row (note that the RS is reverse stockinette for color B); ssk, knit to last 2 sts, k2tog, return the 54 held left sleeve cap sts onto empty needle preparing to

work a RS row; pm, ssk, knit to last 2 sts, k2tog—104 sts; 52 sts each side of m.

ROW 1 (WS): Purl to 2 sts before m, ssp, sl m, p2tog, purl to end—2 sts dec'd.

ROW 2 (RS): Ssk, knit to 2 sts before m, k2tog, sl m, ssk, knit to last 2 sts, k2tog—4 sts dec'd.

Rep the last 2 rows 15 times—8 sts rem.

LAST ROW (WS): P2tog, ssp, sl m, p2tog, ssp—4 sts rem.

Break yarn leaving an 8" (20.5 cm) tail and thread end onto a yarn

It's easy to adjust the length of a "top-down" sleeve, but the unusual construction of this design might have you scratching your head a bit. To test the length as you knit the sleeve, work the sleeve to the halfway point where the color changes, then sew the sleeve closed for a few inches at the top. Try the sleeve on: The middle triangle on the strip should be centered on your back, with the upper edge connecting one shoulder tip to the other. This should give you a good idea of how the sleeve will fall on your body when the cardigan is finished.

needle. Run the needle through the rem sts twice to cinch them together. Secure end.

Sleeve

Carefully remove waste yarn from provisional CO of one sleeve and place 56 (62, 70, 76, 84) sts onto needle and join color B preparing to work a RS row (note that the RS is reverse stockinette for color B).

NEXT ROW (RS): Purl.

Work 13 (11, 7, 7, 7) rows even in Rev St st (purl on RS, knit on WS), ending after a WS row.

DEC ROW (RS): P1, ssp, purl to last 3 sts, p2tog, p1—2 sts dec'd.

Rep the last 14 (12, 8, 8, 8) rows 3 (3, 6, 6, 6) times—48 (54, 56, 62, 70) sts rem.

Work even in Rev St st until 60 rows are worked on sleeve.

Break yarn for color B and join color A.

Work 10 (0, 4, 4, 4) rows even in St st (knit on RS, purl on WS).

DEC ROW (RS): K1, ssk, knit to last 3 sts, k2tog, k1—2 sts dec'd.

Work 13 (11, 7, 7, 7) rows even in St st (knit on RS, purl on WS), ending after a WS row.

Rep the last 14 (12, 8, 8, 8) rows 2 (4, 4, 5, 6) times—42 (44, 46, 50, 56) sts.

Cont working even in St st until sleeve meas 18½" (47 cm) from pick-up row, ending after a WS row.

Break yarn for color A and join color B. Knit 1 RS row.

Work in 1 × 1 Rib for 3" (7.5 cm)

BO loosely in rib.

Make second sleeve the same as the first.

Finishing

Block pieces to measurements.

Sew The Strips Together

Using a yarn needle, sew the sleeve seams together from the cuff to the provisional cast-on using the mattress stitch (match the color of yarn threaded on the needle to the section you are sewing on the sleeve). Arrange the pieces as they appear in the schematic, being careful that all the RS's are facing up. Thread a yarn needle with a long length of yarn (the color doesn't matter), and sew the 3 strips together using the mattress stitch.

Long Edging

Arrange cardigan so the RS is facing you with one of the long edges at the top. With long circular needles and color A, beg at right corner of a long edge, pick up and knit 188 (210, 222, 232, 256) sts along edge.

Work in 1 × 1 Rib for 6 rows.

BO loosely in rib.

Rep at the other long edge.

Short Edging

Arrange cardigan so the RS is facing you with one of the short edges at the top. With long circular needles and color A, beg at right corner of a short edge, pick up and knit 6 sts from the long edging, 120 sts along the short edge, then 6 sts from the long edging—132 sts.

Work in 1 × 1 Rib for 6 rows.

BO loosely in rib.

Rep at the other short edge.

Button Loops

With crochet hook, draw a loop through the tip of one top corner of the edging, make a chain about 1¼" (3.2 cm) long. Fold the loop down diagonally toward the center of the cardigan, and secure end of the chain on the WS of the cardigan to create a button loop. Rep at the other top corner.

Sew 2 buttons to the WS, on the seam allowance between the top and middle strips, approximately 6" (15 cm) from the center on either side (12" [30.5 cm] apart).

Weave in ends and block again if desired.

sweetness
pullover

THIS YOKE-STYLE PULLOVER is knitted from the top down and features a cute dotted colorwork pattern around the shoulders. Top-down construction makes the length very easy to adjust for both the body and the sleeves.

FINISHED SIZE
32¼ (39½, 44, 48, 52¾)" (82 [100.5, 112, 122, 134] cm) bust circumference.

Pullover shown measures 32¼" (82 cm).

YARN
Sport (#2 Fine)

Shown here: Madelinetosh Tosh Sport (100% superwash merino wool; 270 yd [247m]/100 g): Cloak (A) 4 (4, 5, 5, 6) skeins; Pop Rocks (B), 1 skein; Maple Leaf Green (C), 1 skein.

NEEDLES
Body: Size U.S. 4 (3.5 mm): 24" (60 cm) circular needle (cir) and set of 4 double pointed (dpn).

Ribbing: Size U.S. 3 (3.25 mm): 24" (60 cm) cir and set of 4 dpn.

Adjust needle sizes if necessary to obtain the correct gauge.

NOTIONS
Stitch markers (m)

Stitch holders or waste yarn

Yarn needle

GAUGE
20 sts and 30 rnds = 4" (10 cm) in stockinette st.

Yoke

With color A and smaller cir, CO 128 (136, 146, 154, 162) sts. Join to work in the rnd, being careful not to twist sts and place marker (pm) for beg of rnd.

NEXT 4 RNDS: *K1, p1; rep from *.

Change to the larger cir and knit 1 rnd.

Raise Back of Neck

The back of the neck is raised using short-row shaping (see Techniques). If you prefer a reversible sweater or a lower back, you can skip ahead to the next section.

SHORT-ROW 1 (RS): K48 (52, 57, 61, 65), w&t.

SHORT-ROW 2 (WS): Purl to m, w&t;

SHORT-ROW 3 (RS): Knit to wrapped st from the previous row, knit the wrapped st incorporating the wrap, k5, w&t;

SHORT-ROW 4 (WS): Purl to the wrapped st from the previous row, purl the wrapped st incorporating the wrap, p5, w&t;

Rep the last 2 short-rows 3 (4, 4, 4, 5) times.

NEXT ROW (RS): Knit to m.

NEXT RND: Knit, incorporating the last 2 wraps from the previous short-rows as you pass them.

Shape Yoke

The yoke is worked in St st (knit all sts every rnd) and gets its wide conical shape from 4 increase rnds. The increase rnds are placed between 2 sections of Fair Isle color work. Between the color work sections, carry the unused colors along the back side by loosely twisting them together once with the used color at the start of each row.

Fair Isle patterns get a small jog at the start of the row when they are worked in the rnd, so the beg of rnds is offset to behind the shoulder for a more attractive look.

MOVE BEG OF RNDS: Remove beg of rnd m, k5 (6, 6, 7, 7), replace m.

Knit 2 rnds.

INC RND 1: K2 (3, 6, 0, 0), *M1, k4 (3, 3, 3, 3), M1, k5 (4, 4, 4, 3); rep from * —156 (174, 186, 198, 216) sts.

Join colors B and C and work Rnds 1–12 of Colorwork Chart.

INC RND 2: With color A, k4 (6, 2, 2, 0), *M1, k4, M1, k4 (4, 4, 3, 4); rep from * —194 (216, 232, 254, 270) sts.

Knit 8 rnds.

INC RND 3: K7 (0, 4, 1, 0), *M1, k5 (6, 6, 5, 5), M1, k6 (6, 6, 6, 5); rep from * —228 (252, 270, 300, 324) sts.

Work Rnds 1–17 of Colorwork Chart. Break colors B and C and cont working the rest of the sweater in color A.

Knit 1 rnd.

COLORWORK CHART

☐	with color A, knit
−	with color B, knit
I	with color C, knit
☐	pattern repeat

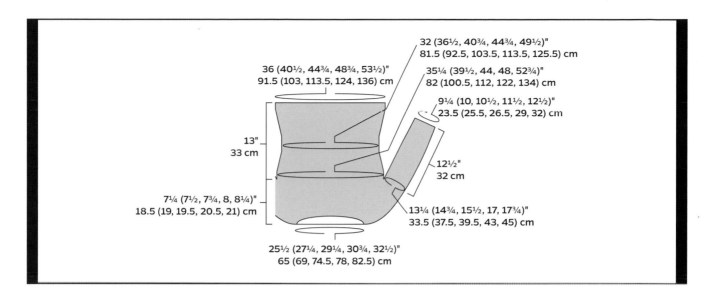

36 (40½, 44¾, 48¾, 53½)"
91.5 (103, 113.5, 124, 136) cm

32 (36½, 40¾, 44¾, 49½)"
81.5 (92.5, 103.5, 113.5, 125.5) cm

35¼ (39½, 44, 48, 52¾)"
82 (100.5, 112, 122, 134) cm

9¼ (10, 10½, 11½, 12½)"
23.5 (25.5, 26.5, 29, 32) cm

13"
33 cm

12½"
32 cm

7¼ (7½, 7¾, 8, 8¼)"
18.5 (19, 19.5, 20.5, 21) cm

13¼ (14¾, 15½, 17, 17¾)"
33.5 (37.5, 39.5, 43, 45) cm

25½ (27¼, 29¼, 30¾, 32½)"
65 (69, 74.5, 78, 82.5) cm

INC RND 4: K4 (5, 6, 3, 0), *M1, k7 (6, 5, 5, 6), M1, k7 (7, 6, 6, 6); rep from *—260 (290, 318, 354, 378) sts

Knit 5 (6, 8, 11, 12) rnds.

DIVIDE SLEEVES AND BODY: *K76 (85, 98, 106, 116), put the next 54 (60, 63, 71, 73) sts on a st holder or waste yarn for sleeve, use the backward loop method (see Techniques) to CO 12 (14, 14, 14, 16) sts for the underarm; rep from *—176 (198, 220, 240, 264) sts rem.

Body

PLACE MARKERS FOR WAIST SHAPING: Remove beg of rnd m, k16 (18, 21, 23, 25) sts, pm, k44 (49, 54, 60, 66), pm, k44 (50, 56, 60, 66), pm, k44 (49, 54, 60, 66), pm, k22 (25, 28, 30, 33) sts, place a new beg of rnd m.

Shape Waist

Knit 7 rnds.

DEC RND: *Knit to 2 sts before m, k2tog, sl m, knit to next m, sl m, ssk; rep from *—4 sts dec'd.

Rep the last 8 rnds 3 times—160 (182, 204, 224, 248) sts rem.

Knit 20 rnds (subtract extra length here if you are short-waisted).

INC RND: *Knit to m, M1, sl m, knit to next m, sl m, M1; rep from *—4 sts inc'd.

Knit 7 rnds.

Rep the last 8 rnds 3 times, then work Inc Rnd once more—180 (202, 224, 244, 268) sts.

Work even in St st until piece meas 12½" (31.5 cm) from divide.

Change to smaller size cir.

NEXT 4 RNDS: *K1, p1; rep from *.

BO loosely in rib.

Sleeve

Divide 54 (60, 63, 71, 73) held sts from one sleeve evenly onto 3 larger dpn. With another dpn and color A, beg at center of underarm, pick up and knit 6 (7, 7, 7, 8) sts from the CO underarm sts, knit to end of held sts, pick up and knit 6 (7, 7, 7, 8) sts from the rest of the underarm sts, pm and join to work in the rnd—66 (74, 77, 85, 89) sts.

Knit 7 (6, 6, 5, 5) rnds.

DEC RND: K1, ssk, knit to last 2 sts, k2tog—2 sts dec'd.

Rep the last 8 (7, 7, 6, 6) rnds 9 (11, 11, 12, 12) times—46 (50, 53, 59, 63) sts rem.

Work even in St st until the sleeve meas 12" (30.5 cm) from divide.

Change to smaller dpn

Sizes 44 (48, 52¾)" only:

DEC RND: K2tog, *p1, k1; rep from *52 (58, 62) sts rem.

All Sizes:

NEXT 4 (4, 3, 3, 3) RNDS: *K1, p1; rep from *.

BO loosely in rib.

Make second sleeve the same as the first.

Finishing

Weave in the loose ends. Block to finished measurements.

germander
shrug

THIS ELEGANT, LOOSE-FITTING SHRUG can be worn in a variety of ways to suit your taste: thrown on quickly with an open fluttering front; with the collar folded down for a smarter look; or even upside down, which lengthens the back to display the full lace panel. The design features a striking lace vine motif on the back, easy drop-shoulder sleeve construction, and textured Seed stitch borders.

FINISHED SIZE

About 32 (36, 40, 44, 48)" (81.5 [91.5, 101.5, 112, 122] cm) bust circumference.

Shrug shown measures 36" (91.5 cm).

Note. The open front makes the fit very loose, so if you are between sizes, select the smaller size.

YARN

Worsted (#4 Medium)

Shown here: Louet Gems Light/Worsted (100% merino; 175 yd [160 m]/100 g): #54 Teal, 4 (4, 4, 5, 5) skeins.

NEEDLES

Size U.S. 8 (5 mm): straight.

Adjust needle size if necessary to obtain the correct gauge.

NOTIONS

Stitch markers (m)

Removable stitch markers

Smooth waste yarn for provisional cast-on

Yarn needle

GAUGE

16½ sts and 24½ rows = 4" (10 cm) in St st.

17 sts and 23 rows = 4" (10 cm) in Lace Chart.

Notes
The back is worked from the center outward toward the shoulders. This is to make the increases and decreases of the lace pattern on the right and left sides mirror perfectly. For a seamless look, I recommend using a provisional cast-on.

Left Back

Use a provisional method (see Techniques) to CO 92 sts.

NEXT ROW (WS): [K1, p1] 3 times, purl to last 6 sts, [p1, k1] 3 times.

Work Rows 1–39 of Lace Chart.

NEXT ROW (WS): [K1, p1] 3 times, purl to last 6 sts, [p1, k1] 3 times.

NEXT ROW (RS): [K1, p1] 3 times, knit to last 6 sts, [p1, k1] 3 times.

Rep the last 2 rows until the piece meas 8 (9, 10, 11, 12)" (20.5 [23, 25.5, 28, 30.5] cm) from CO, ending after a RS row.

NEXT ROW (WS): BO 46 sts for side of body and armhole, purl to last 6 sts, pm, [p1, k1] 3 times—46 sts rem.

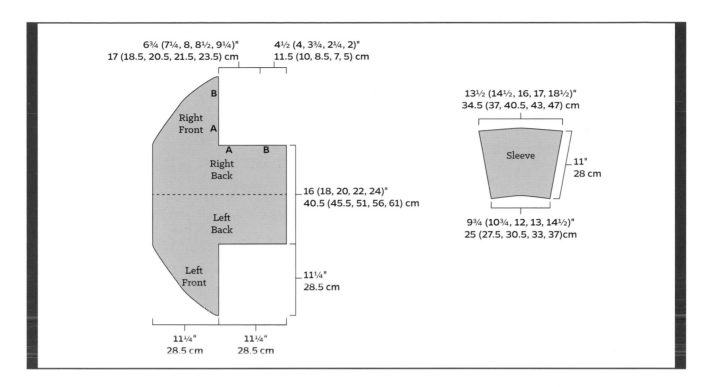

6¾ (7¼, 8, 8½, 9¼)"
17 (18.5, 20.5, 21.5, 23.5) cm

4½ (4, 3¾, 2¼, 2)"
11.5 (10, 8.5, 7, 5) cm

B
Right Front A

A B
Right Back

16 (18, 20, 22, 24)"
40.5 (45.5, 51, 56, 61) cm

Left Back

Left Front

11¼"
28.5 cm

11¼"
28.5 cm

11¼"
28.5 cm

13½ (14½, 16, 17, 18½)"
34.5 (37, 40.5, 43, 47) cm

Sleeve

11"
28 cm

9¾ (10¾, 12, 13, 14½)"
25 (27.5, 30.5, 33, 37)cm

Left Front
Shape Front

DEC ROW (RS): [K1, p1] 3 times, sl m, ssk, knit to end—1 st dec'd.

NEXT ROW (WS): Purl to m, sl m, [k1, p1] 3 times.

Rep the last 2 rows 19 times—26 sts rem.

DEC ROW (RS): [K1, p1] 3 times, sl m, ssk, knit to end—1 st dec'd.

DEC ROW (WS): Purl to 2 sts before m, ssp, sl m, [k1, p1] 3 times—1 st dec'd.

Rep the last 2 rows 8 times—8 sts rem.

BO all sts.

Right Back

Carefully remove waste yarn from provisional CO placing 92 sts onto needle and join yarn preparing to work a WS row.

NEXT ROW (WS): [K1, p1] 3 times, purl to last 6 sts, [p1, k1] 3 times.

Work Rows 1–39 of Lace Chart.

NEXT ROW (WS): [K1, p1] 3 times, purl to last 6 sts, [p1, k1] 3 times.

NEXT ROW (RS): [K1, p1] 3 times, knit to last 6 sts, [p1, k1] 3 times.

Rep the last 2 rows until the piece meas 8 (9, 10, 11, 12)" (20.5 [23, 25.5, 28, 30.5] cm) from CO, ending after a WS row.

NEXT ROW (RS): BO 46 sts for side of body and armhole, knit to last 6 sts, pm, [p1, k1] 3 times—46 sts rem.

Right Front
Shape Front

NEXT ROW (WS): [K1, p1] 3 times, sl m, purl to end.

DEC ROW (RS): Knit to 2 sts before m, k2tog, sl m [p1, k1] 3 times—1 st dec'd.

Rep the last 2 rows 19 times—26 sts rem.

DEC ROW (WS): [K1, p1] 3 times, sl m, p2tog, purl to end—1 st dec'd.

DEC ROW (RS): Knit to 2 sts before m, k2tog, sl m, [p1, k1] 3 times—1 st dec'd.

Rep the last 2 rows 8 times—8 sts rem.

BO all sts.

LACE CHART

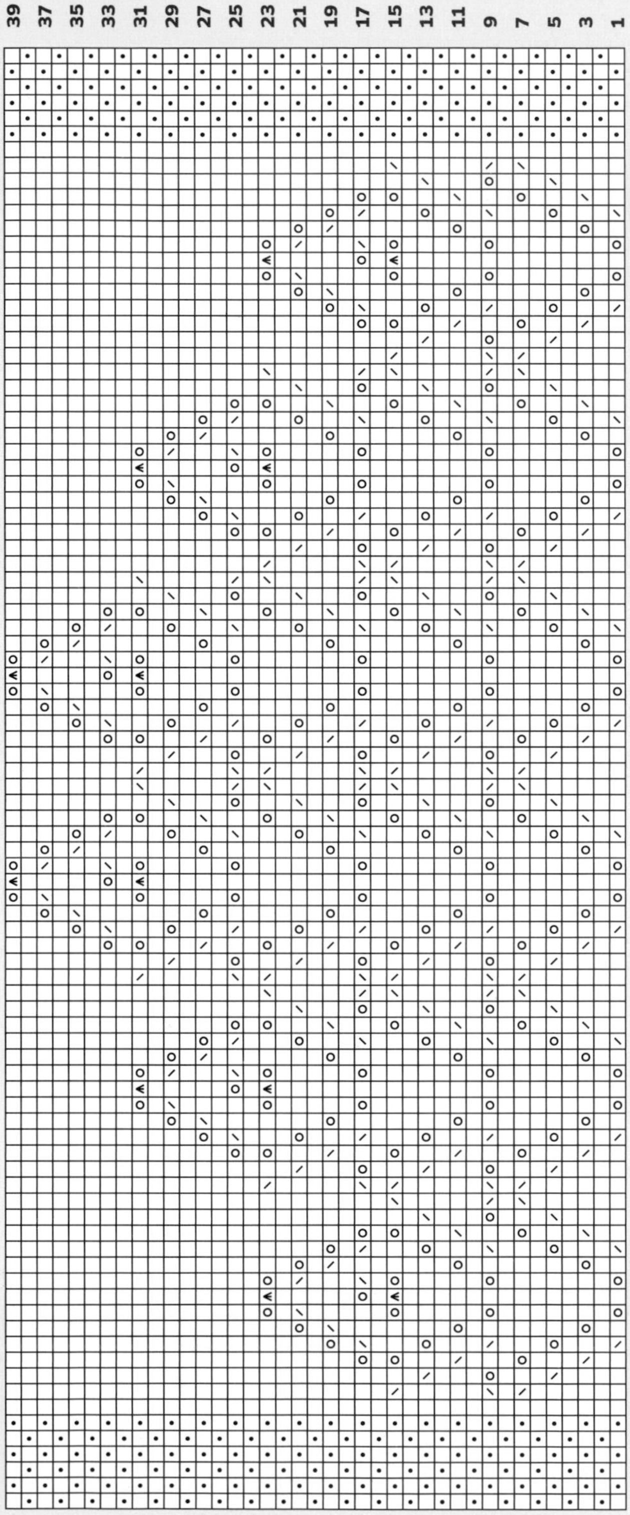

- knit on RS, purl on WS
- purl on RS, knit on WS
- yo
- ssk
- k2tog
- s2kp

Sleeve

CO 56 (60, 66, 70, 76) sts.

SET-UP ROW (RS): K28 (30, 33, 35, 38), pm, knit to end.

Work 9 rows even in St st.

DEC ROW (RS): K1, ssk, knit to 2 sts before m, k2tog, sl m, ssk, knit to last 3 sts, k2tog, k1—4 sts dec'd.

Rep the last 10 rows 3 times—40 (44, 50, 54, 60) sts rem.

Remove m as you work the next row.

Work even in St st (knit on RS, purl on WS) until the sleeve meas 9½" (24 cm) from CO.

Work 12 rows even in Seed St.

Bind off in Seed St.

Work second sleeve the same as the first.

Finishing

Block pieces to measurements.

Fold the fronts down so the straight selvedge edges line up with the BO side/armhole edge of the back. Place removable marker into fabric 6¾ (7¼, 8, 8½, 9¼). (17 [18.5, 20.5, 21.5, 23.5] cm) down from the fold. The space between the m and the fold (marked as A on schematic) is for the armhole, the space below the m and the lower edge is the side body (marked B on schematic). Fold the sleeve in half lengthwise with RS facing out. Align the fold on the sleeve with the fold on body, with CO edge of sleeve against body. Thread a long length of yarn onto the yarn needle, and using mattress stitch, sew the sleeves to body between the fold and marker. With another length of yarn, sew the sleeve seam beg at the cuff, and working to the underarm, then cont the seam down the side of the body, aligning the BO edge of the front with the Seed St on the back selvedge edge. Rep on the other side.

Weave in the ends.

Block again if desired.

burren
pullover

THIS SEAMLESS, REVERSIBLE CROPPED sweater has a yoke shoulder construction to showcase asymmetrical tapering stripes between the increase rows. The wide neckline and short length make this a fun layering piece to wear off the shoulder, and looks great paired with a high-waisted skirt or close-fitting pants.

FINISHED SIZE

About 32½ (37, 41¾, 45¼, 50¼). (82.5 [94, 106, 115, 127.5] cm) bust circumference.

Pullover shown measures 37" (94 cm).

YARN

Chunky (#5 Bulky)

Shown here: Berroco Kodiak (61% alpaca, 24% nylon, 15% wool; 125 yd [115 m]/50 g): #7014 Glacier (A), 1 skein; #7040 Alpine (B), 3 (3, 3, 4, 4) skeins; #7005 Weasel (C), 1 skein; #7007 Harbor Seal (D), 1 skein.

NEEDLES

Size U.S. 10½ (6.5 mm): 24" (60 cm) circular (cir) and set of 4 double-pointed (dpn).

Adjust needle size if necessary to obtain the correct gauge.

NOTIONS

Stitch markers (m)

Stitch holders or waste yarn

Yarn needle

GAUGE

14 sts and 21 rnds = 4" (10 cm) in stockinette stitch.

Yoke

With color A and cir, CO 88 (94, 102, 110, 116) sts. Join to work in the rnd, being careful not to twist sts and place marker (pm) for beg of rnd.

NEXT 2 RNDS: Knit.

NEXT 4 RNDS: *K1, p1; rep from *.

The rest of the sweater is worked in St st (knit all sts, every rnd) until the hem and cuffs.

INC RND 1: K3 (4, 4, 6, 6), *M1, k5 (5, 5, 5, 3), M1, k6 (5, 5, 4, 4), M1, k6 (5, 4, 4, 4); rep from *—103 (112, 123, 134, 146) sts.

Knit 2 rnds, then break color A.

Change to color B and knit 3 rnds.

INC RND 2: K1 (0, 3, 6, 2), *M1, k5 (5, 5, 5, 6), M1, k6 (5, 5, 5, 6), M1, k6 (6, 5, 6, 6); rep from *—121 (133, 147, 158, 170) sts.

Beg Short-Rows (see Techniques):

SHORT-ROW 1 (RS): Knit to last 14 (17, 19, 19, 20) sts, w&t;

SHORT-ROW 2 (WS): Purl to last 14 (17, 19, 19, 20) sts, w&t;

SHORT-ROW 3 (RS): Knit to 8 (8, 7, 8, 9) sts before the wrapped st from the previous row, w&t;

SHORT-ROW 4 (WS): Purl to 8 (8, 7, 8, 9) sts before the wrapped st from the previous row, w&t;

Rep the last 2 short-rows 3 (3, 4, 4, 4) times—29 (35, 39, 40, 40) sts rem unwrapped in center.

END SHORT-ROWS (RS): Knit to the end, incorporating the wraps as you pass them—15 (15, 17, 17, 17) rows of color B on the thickest part of the stripe and 5 rows on the narrowest part of the stripe.

Break color B.

MOVE BEG OF RNDS: Remove the beg of rnd m, with color C k60 (66, 73, 79, 85) incorporating the wraps as you pass them, replace beg of rnd m.

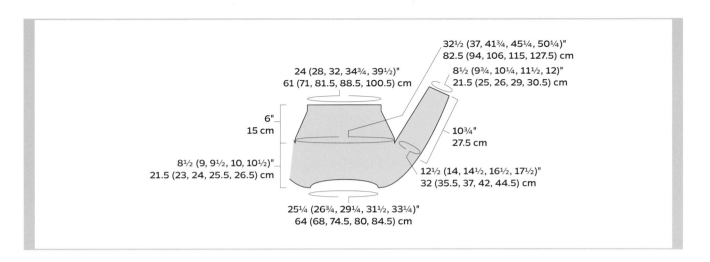

Figure measurements:
- 32½ (37, 41¾, 45¼, 50¼)" 82.5 (94, 106, 115, 127.5) cm
- 8½ (9¾, 10¼, 11½, 12)" 21.5 (25, 26, 29, 30.5) cm
- 24 (28, 32, 34¾, 39½)" 61 (71, 81.5, 88.5, 100.5) cm
- 6" 15 cm
- 10¾" 27.5 cm
- 8½ (9, 9½, 10, 10½)" 21.5 (23, 24, 25.5, 26.5) cm
- 12½ (14, 14½, 16½, 17½)" 32 (35.5, 37, 42, 44.5) cm
- 25¼ (26¾, 29¼, 31½, 33¼)" 64 (68, 74.5, 80, 84.5) cm

Beg Short-Rows:

SHORT-ROW 1 (RS): K75 (84, 93, 99, 105), w&t;

SHORT-ROW 2 (WS): P29 (35, 39, 40, 40), w&t;

SHORT-ROW 3 (RS): Knit to the wrapped st from the previous row, k1 incorporating wrap, k7 (7, 6, 7, 8), w&t;

SHORT-ROW 4 (WS): Purl to the wrapped st from the previous row, p1 incorporating wrap, p7 (7, 6, 7, 8), w&t;

Rep the last 2 short-rows 3 (3, 4, 4, 4) times—14 (17, 19, 19, 20) sts rem unwrapped at each end of row.

END SHORT-ROWS (RS): Knit to the end, incorporating the wrap as you pass it—11 (11, 13, 13, 13) rows of color C on the thickest part of the stripe and 1 row at the narrowest part of the stripe.

INC RND 3: K4 (7, 4, 2, 2), *M1, k6 (7, 6, 6, 6), M1, k7 (7, 7, 6, 6); rep from * —139 (151, 169, 184, 198) sts.

Knit 3 rnds, then break color C.

Change to color D and knit 3 rnds.

INC RND 4: K3 (1, 4, 2, 3), *M1, k8 (7, 7, 7, 7), M1, k9 (8, 8, 7, 8); rep from * —155 (171, 191, 210, 224) sts.

Beg Short-Rows:

SHORT-ROW 1 (RS): Knit to last 19 (21, 23, 25, 28) sts, w&t;

SHORT-ROW 2 (WS): Purl to last 19 (21, 23, 25, 28) sts, w&t;

SHORT-ROW 3 (RS): Knit to 10 (11, 10, 11, 11) sts before the wrapped st from the previous row, w&t;

SHORT-ROW 4 (WS): Purl to 10 (11, 10, 11, 11) sts before the wrapped st from the previous row, w&t;

Rep the last 2 short-rows 3 (3, 4, 4, 4) times—37 (41, 45, 50, 58) sts rem unwrapped in center.

END SHORT-ROWS (RS): Knit to the end, incorporating the wraps as you pass them—15 (15, 17, 17, 17) rows of color D on the thickest part of the stripe and 5 rows on the narrowest part of the stripe.

Break color D.

MOVE BEG OF RNDS: Remove the beg of rnd m, with color A k77 (85, 95, 105, 112) incorporating the wraps as you pass them, replace beg of rnd m.

Beg Short-Rows:

SHORT-ROW 1 (RS): K96 (106, 118, 130, 141), w&t;

SHORT-ROW 2 (WS): P37 (41, 45, 50, 58), w&t;

SHORT-ROW 3 (RS): Knit to the wrapped st from the previous row, k1 incorporating wrap, k9 (10, 9, 10, 10), w&t;

SHORT-ROW 4 (WS): Purl to the wrapped st from the previous row, p1 incorporating wrap, p9 (10, 9, 10, 10), w&t;

Rep the last 2 short-rows 3 (3, 4, 4, 4) times—19 (21, 23, 25, 28) sts rem unwrapped at each end of row.

END SHORT-ROWS (RS): Knit to the end, incorporating the wrap as you pass it—11 (11, 13, 13, 13) rows of color A on the thickest part of the stripe and 1 row at the narrowest part of the stripe.

INC RND 5: K0 (3, 2, 2, 4), *M1, k11 (8, 9, 8, 7), M1, k10 (8, 9, 9, 7), M1, k10 (8, 9, 9, 8); rep from *—170 (192, 212, 234, 254) sts.

Knit 3 rnds. Break color A.

Change to color B and knit 2 (4, 5, 8, 10) rnds.

Divide for Body

NEXT RND: Remove beg of rnd m, k18 (20, 21, 24, 25), replace beg of rnd m, k49 (56, 64, 69, 77), pm, put the next 36 (40, 42, 48, 50) sts on a st holder or waste yarn for sleeve, use the backward loop method (see Techniques) to CO 8 (9, 9, 10, 11) sts for the underarm, pm, k49 (56, 64, 69, 77), pm, put the rem 36 (40, 42, 48, 50) sts on a st holder or waste yarn for sleeve, CO 8 (9, 9, 10, 11) sts for the underarm—114 (130, 146, 158, 176) sts rem.

Body

Knit 3 rnds.

Shape Sides

DEC RND: *Ssk, knit to 2 sts before the next m, k2tog, sl m, knit to next m, sl m; rep from * once more, knit to end—4 sts dec'd.

Knit 5 rnds.

Rep the last 6 rnds 2 times, then work Dec Rnd again—98 (114, 130, 142, 160) sts rem.

> **Note:** *for smallest size, the last Dec Rnd requires a stitch to be borrowed from outside the markers to complete the decreases.*

Knit 2 rnds.

DEC FOR RIBBING: K0 (2, 4, 2, 6), *k2tog, k5; rep from *—84 (98, 112, 122, 138) sts rem.

NEXT 4 RNDS: *K1, p1; rep from *.

Jogless Stripes In The Round

Because circular knitting is really knitting in a spiral, there will always be a little stair step, or "jog," where you switch colors for a stripe.

Here's a little trick to hide the jog (this works best when you're making stripes that are at least 3 rnds thick):

1. Switch colors when you are instructed to in the pattern and work 1 rnd normally.

2. Before you knit the first st of the second rnd, use your right needle to pull the st just below that first st up onto the tip of the left needle, being careful not to twist it as you do.

3. Knit the lifted st together with the regular first st as if they were one. Continue knitting as you would normally. After a couple of rows, you'll see that the jog in the stripes has become nearly invisible.

NEXT 2 RNDS: Knit.

BO very loosely, kwise.

Sleeve

Divide held sts from one sleeve evenly over 3 dpn. With another dpn and color B and dpn, beg at center of underarm, pick up and knit 4 (5, 5, 5, 6) sts from the CO underarm sts, knit to end of held sts, pick up and knit 4 (4, 4, 5, 5) sts from the rest of the underarm sts, pm and join to work in the rnd—44 (49, 51, 58, 61) sts.

Knit 1 (1, 1, 4, 4) rnds.

Shape Sleeve

DEC RND: Ssk, knit to last 2 sts, k2tog—2 sts dec'd.

Knit 6 (6, 6, 4, 4) rnds.

Rep the last 7 (7, 7, 5, 5) rnds 5 (5, 5, 7, 7) times, then work Dec Rnd once more—30 (35, 37, 40, 43) sts rem.

Knit 6 (5, 5, 5, 4) rnds.

Sizes 37 (41¾, 50¼). only:

DEC RND: K2tog, knit to end—1 st dec'd.

All Sizes:

NEXT 4 RNDS: *K1, p1; rep from *.

NEXT 2 RNDS: Knit.

BO very loosely, kwise.

Work second sleeve the same as the first.

Finishing

Weave in the ends. Block to the measurements.

laszlo
cardigan

THIS LONG, ELEGANT CARDIGAN features a bold graduating stripe pattern in the yoke style shoulders, a wide draped collar, and button details at the cuffs and pockets. It's worked seamlessly from the top down in one piece, making it easy for you to adjust the length. The optional patch pockets are attached at the end.

FINISHED SIZE

About 32 (37, 40, 45, 47½)" (81.5 [94, 101.5, 114.5, 120.5] cm) bust circumference, buttoned.

Cardigan shown measures 37" (94 cm).

YARN

Worsted (#4 Medium)

Shown here: The Fibre Company Canopy Worsted (50% baby alpaca, 30% merino wool, 20% viscose from bamboo; 200 yd [183 m]/100 g): Obsidian (A), 3 skeins; Orchid (B), 4 (5, 5, 6, 6) skeins.

NEEDLES

Body: Size U.S. 8 (5 mm): 24" (60 cm) circular (cir) and set of 4 or 5 double-pointed (dpn).

Ribbing: Size U.S. 7 (4.5 mm): 24" (60 cm) cir and dpn.

Pockets: Sizes U.S. 7 and 8 (4.5 and 5 mm): straight.

Adjust needle size if necessary to obtain the correct gauge.

NOTIONS

Stitch markers (m)

2 removable stitch markers

Stitch holders or waste yarn

Yarn needle

Twenty-four ⅝" (1.5 cm) buttons

Sewing needle (for buttons)

Matching thread (for buttons)

GAUGE

18 sts and 25 rows = 4" (10 cm) in St st with larger needles.

Stitch Guide

Yoke Stripe Pattern (any number of sts):
With color A, work 7 (9, 13, 15, 17) rows.

Change to color B, work 6 rows.

Change to color A, work 22 rows.

Change to color B, work 10 rows.

Change to color A, work 14 rows.

Change to color B, work the last 2 rows of the yoke.

Sleeve Stripe Pattern (any number of sts):
With color B, work 11 rnds. (Including rows from yoke, there should be 14 rows of color B total in this stripe.)

Change to color A, work 10 rnds.

Change to color B, work 22 rnds.

Change to color A, work 6 rnds.

Change to color B for the rest of the sleeve.

1 × 1 Rib:
(multiple of 2 sts)

ROW 1: *K1, p1; rep from *.

REP ROW 1 FOR PATT.

(multiple of 2 sts + 1)

ROW 1: K1, *p1, k1; rep from *.

ROW 2: P1, *k1, p1; rep from *.

Rep Rows 1 and 2 for patt.

Notes

Body and sleeves are knitted from the top down seamlessly in one big piece. The collar and front edging sts are picked up from the body. The pockets are knit separately, and attached at the end.

Pick Up and Purl: *This technique is used on the front edging where the collar flips and you can see the inside. To change from "Pick Up and Knit" to "Pick Up and Purl," simply bring the yarn to the front between the tips of your needles, and begin picking up sts from the back side of the fabric instead of the front. Because the edging is a contrasting color, you will see the point where you changed the yarn to the front. Minimize this by pulling the yarn tightly as you create your first purl st. It shouldn't be too noticeable, but if you're a perfectionist, you can use a duplicate st to hide the tiny wrap around the edge.*

When you pick up sts for the collar and edging, pick them up 1 st away from the edge.

Circular needle is used to accommodate large number of sts. Do not join; work back and forth in rows.

Yoke

With color A and larger cir, CO 31 (34, 41, 42, 44) sts. Do not join; work back and forth in rows.

Beg working Yoke Stripe Patt, and at the same time, work as foll:

NEXT ROW (WS): Purl.

Work 4 rows in St st (knit on RS, purl on WS), ending after a WS row.

Shape Yoke

INC ROW 1 (RS): K1, *M1, k1; rep from * —61 (67, 81, 83, 87) sts.

Work 9 rows even in St st.

INC ROW 2 (RS): K1 (2, 3, 3, 2), *M1, k1, M1, k2, M1, k2 (2, 3, 2, 2) twice; rep from *—97 (106, 120, 131, 138) sts.

Work 9 (9, 9, 11, 11) rows even in St st.

INC ROW 3 (RS): K1 (1, 5, 1, 3), *M1, k3 (2, 2, 2, 2), M1, k3; rep from * —129 (148, 166, 183, 192) sts.

Work 9 (9, 11, 11, 13) rows even in St st.

INC ROW 4 (RS): K3 (1, 6, 3, 8), *M1, k3 (3, 4, 5, 4), M1, k4; rep from *—165 (190, 206, 223, 238) sts.

Work 9 (11, 13, 13, 13) rows even in St st.

Sizes 32 (37, 40, 47½)" only:

INC ROW 5 (RS): K5 (1, 8, 4), *M1, k5 (4, 4, 4), M1, k5; rep from *—197 (232, 250, 290) sts.

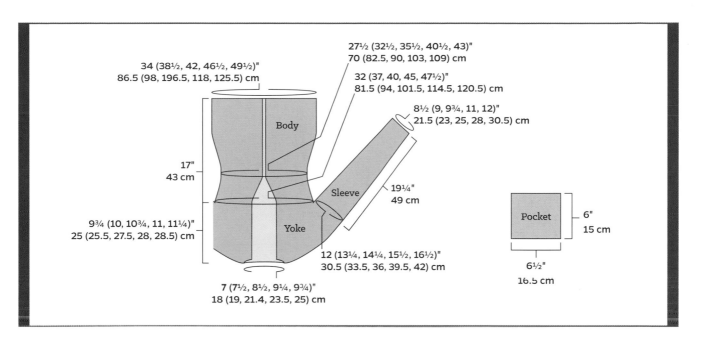

34 (38½, 42, 46½, 49½)"
86.5 (98, 196.5, 118, 125.5) cm

27½ (32½, 35½, 40½, 43)"
70 (82.5, 90, 103, 109) cm

32 (37, 40, 45, 47½)"
81.5 (94, 101.5, 114.5, 120.5) cm

8½ (9, 9¾, 11, 12)"
21.5 (23, 25, 28, 30.5) cm

Body

17"
43 cm

Sleeve

19¼"
49 cm

9¾ (10, 10¾, 11, 11¼)"
25 (25.5, 27.5, 28, 28.5) cm

Yoke

12 (13¼, 14¼, 15½, 16½)"
30.5 (33.5, 36, 39.5, 42) cm

7 (7½, 8½, 9¼, 9¾)"
18 (19, 21.4, 23.5, 25) cm

Pocket

6"
15 cm

6½"
16.5 cm

Size 45" only:

INC ROW 5 (RS): K3, *M1, k4; rep from *
—278 sts.

All Sizes:

Work 15 rows even in St st.

DIVIDE BODY AND SLEEVES (RS):
K22 (28, 31, 35, 37), put the next
45 (51, 54, 59, 61) sts onto a st
holder or waste yarn for sleeve, use
the backward loop method (see
Techniques) to CO 9 (9, 10, 11, 13) sts,
k63 (74, 80, 90, 94), put the next 45
(51, 54, 59, 61) sts onto a st holder
or waste yarn for sleeve, CO 9 (9, 10,
11, 13) sts, knit rem 22 (28, 31, 35, 37)
sts—125 (148, 162, 182, 194) sts rem
for body.

Body

Cont working in color B as foll:

Shape Waist and Neck

SET-UP ROW (WS): P44 (52, 57, 65, 70),
pm, p37 (44, 48, 52, 54), pm, p44
(52, 57, 65, 70) sts.

SHAPING ROW (RS): K1, M1, knit to 2 sts before m, k2tog, sl m, knit to m, sl m, ssk, knit to last st, M1, k1.

Work 5 rows even in St st.

Rep the last 6 rows 3 times, then work shaping row once more—125 (148, 162, 182, 194) sts; 49 (57, 62, 70, 75) sts outside markers on each side, 27 (34, 38, 42, 44) sts between markers.

Place a removable m into the first and last st of the row. You will use these markers later when you pick up sts for the collar.

Work 8 rows even in St st (add length here if you are long-waisted), ending after a RS row.

Shape Hips

SET-UP ROW (WS): P18 (22, 23, 25, 26), pm, purl to the last m, p31 (35, 39, 45, 49), pm, p18 (22, 23, 25, 26) sts.

INC ROW (RS): [Knit to m, sl m, M1, knit to m, M1, sl m] twice, knit to end—4 sts inc'd.

Work 5 rows even in St st.

Rep the last 6 rows 5 times, then work Inc Row once more—153 (176, 190, 210, 222) sts.

Work 11 rows even in St st (adjust the length here, if desired).

Break yarn for color B, change to color A and work 14 rows even in St st.

Break yarn for color A, change to color B and work 1 row even in St st.

Change to smaller cir and work 7 rows in 1 × 1 Rib.

BO loosely in rib (see sidebar titled "Binding off in Rib St").

Left Sleeve

Return 45 (51, 54, 59, 61) held sts from left sleeve to dpn. With empty dpn and color B, beg at center of underarm, pick up and knit 5 (5, 5, 6, 6) sts from the underarm CO sts, knit to end of held sts, then pick up and knit 4 (4, 5, 5, 7) sts from the rem underarm CO sts, pm for beg of rnd—54 (60, 64, 70, 74) sts.

Beg working Sleeve Stripe Patt, and at the same time, work as foll:

Knit 1 rnd.

Shape Sleeve

DEC RND: Ssk, knit to last 2 sts, k2tog—2 sts dec'd.

Knit 8 (6, 6, 6, 6) rnds.

Rep the last 9 (7, 7, 7, 7) rnds 7 (9, 9, 9, 9) times—38 (40, 44, 50, 54) sts rem.

Cont working even in St st (knit all sts, every rnd) until sleeve meas 12¼" (31 cm) from pick-up rnd.

Cuff

NEXT RND: K20 (22, 24, 26, 28), pm, use the backward loop method to CO 5 sts, turn to work the rest of the sleeve flat in rows, discard the beg of rnd m on the next row as you pass it—43 (45, 49, 55, 59) sts.

Change to smaller dpn.

NEXT ROW (WS): P5, sl m, *k1, p1; rep from *.

NEXT ROW (RS): *K1, p1; rep from * to m, knit to end.

Work 1 more row as est.

BUTTONHOLE ROW (RS): *K1, p1; rep from * to m, sl m, k1, pass the second st on the left needle over the first st and off the needle, kfb, k2.

Work 5 rows even as est.

Rep the last 6 rows 5 times, then work buttonhole row once more.

Work 3 rows even as est.

BO all sts loosely as est.

Right Sleeve

Return 45 (51, 54, 59, 61) held sts from right sleeve to dpn. With empty dpn and color B, beg at center of underarm, pick up and knit 5 (5, 5, 6, 6) sts from the underarm CO sts, knit to end of held sts, then pick up and knit 4 (4, 5, 5, 7) sts from the rem underarm CO sts, pm for beg of rnd—54 (60, 64, 70, 74) sts.

Cont working as for left sleeve to cuff.

Cuff

NEXT ROW: K18 (18, 20, 24, 26), pm for new beg of row, turn to work the rest of the sleeve flat in rows. Remove the old beg of rnd m on the next row as you pass it. The new beg of row m can be removed once pattern is visually est.

Change to smaller dpn.

NEXT ROW (WS): *P1, k1; rep from * to end, pm, use the backward loop method to CO 5 sts—43 (45, 49, 55, 59) sts.

NEXT ROW (RS): Knit to m, *p1, k1; rep from *.

NEXT ROW (WS): *P1, k1; rep from * to m, p5.

Work 2 more rows as est.

BUTTONHOLE ROW (RS): K1, pass the second st on the left needle over the first st and off the needle, kfb, k2, sl m, *p1, k1; rep from *.

Work 5 rows even as est.

Rep the last 6 rnds 5 times, then work buttonhole row once more.

Work 3 rows even as est.

BO all sts loosely as est.

Pocket

With color A, and larger needles, CO 29 sts.

NEXT ROW (RS): Knit.

Work 13 more rows in St st, ending after a WS row.

Change to color B and work 16 more rows even in St st, ending after a WS row.

Change to smaller needles.

Work 4 rows in 1 × 1 Rib, ending after a WS row.

BUTTONHOLE ROW (RS): Work 13 sts in rib as est, pass the second st on the left needle over the first st and off the needle, kfb, work in rib to end.

Work 3 more rows in 1 × 1 Rib as est.

BO in rib.

Make a second pocket the same as the first.

Finishing

Block pieces to measurements.

Collar

With larger cir and color B, pick up and knit 63 (65, 67, 69, 70) sts along the right-front edge between the removable m and the CO edge, pm, pick up and knit 31 (34, 38, 42, 44) sts across neck CO sts, pm, pick

up and knit 63 (65, 67, 69, 70) sts between the CO sts and the other removable m—157 (164, 172, 180, 184) sts.

> **Note:** The collar is worked in rev St st because it will be folded back.

NEXT ROW (WS): K1, ssk, knit to last 3 sts, k2tog, k1—2 sts dec'd.

NEXT ROW (RS): P1, p2tog, purl to last 3 sts, ssp, p1—2 sts dec'd.

Rep the last 2 rows 6 times—129 (136, 144, 152, 156) sts rem.

NECK SHAPING ROW (WS): K1, ssk, knit to m, M1, sl m, knit to m, sl m, M1, knit to last 3 sts, k2tog, k1.

DEC ROW (RS): P1, p2tog, purl to last 3 sts, ssp, p1—2 sts dec'd.

Rep the last 2 rows 5 times—117 (124, 132, 140, 144) sts rem.

Left Front Short-Rows (see Techniques)

SHORT-ROW 1 (WS): K1, ssk, knit to m, remove m, w&t; purl to end—1 st dec'd.

SHORT-ROW 2 (WS): K1, ssk, knit to 3 sts before the wrapped st from the previous row; w&t; purl to end—1 st dec'd.

Rep the last short-row 8 (8, 9, 9, 10) times—107 (114, 121, 129, 132) sts rem; 6 (8, 6, 8, 5) sts rem unwrapped between m and edge.

NEXT ROW (WS): K1, ssk, knit to last 3 sts incorporating the wraps as you pass them, k2tog, k1—105 (112, 122, 127, 130) sts rem.

Right Front Short-Rows

SHORT-ROW 1 (RS): Purl to m, remove m, w&t; knit to last 3 sts before end, k2tog, k1—1 st dec'd.

SHORT-ROW 2 (RS): Purl to 3 st before the wrapped st from the previous row, w&t; knit to last 3 sts, k2tog, k1—1 st dec'd.

Rep the last short-row 8 (8, 9, 9, 10) times—95 (102, 108, 116, 118) sts rem; 5 (7, 5, 7, 4) sts rem unwrapped between m and edge.

NEXT ROW (RS): Break yarn for color B, change to color A, purl to end incorporating the wraps as you pass them.

Change to smaller cir, work 6 rows in 1 × 1 Rib.

BO loosely in rib.

Buttonhole Band

> **Notes:** Sts from body are picked up kwise and sts from collar are picked up pwise (see notes) to keep the pick-up row nice and neat where the collar flips and the inside shows. If you adjusted the length of the body, you will also need to adjust the number of sts you will pick up along the edge of the cardigan.

With RS of the sweater facing, smaller cir and color A, beg at lower edge of right front, pick up and *knit* 58 sts along the right front edge to the collar, pick up and *purl* 50 (50, 52, 52, 54) sts along the collar edge—108 (108, 110, 110, 112) sts.

Work 3 rows in 1 × 1 Rib, ending after a WS row.

BUTTONHOLE ROW (RS): Work 4 (4, 5, 5, 6) sts in rib, *pass the second st on the left needle over the first st and off the needle, kfb, work next 12 sts in rib; rep from * to last 6 (6, 7, 7, 8) sts, pass the second st on the left needle over the first st and off the needle, kfb, work 4 (4, 5, 5, 6) sts in rib—8 buttonholes.

Work 2 rows in 1 × 1 Rib.

BO loosely in rib.

Button Band

With RS of sweater facing, smaller cir and color A, beg at upper collar edge, pick up and *purl* 50 (50, 52, 52, 54) sts along the collar edge, pick up and *knit* 58 sts along the right front edge—108 (108, 110, 110, 112) sts.

Work 6 rows in 1 × 1 Rib.

BO loosely in rib.

Position 8 buttons on the button band, aligning them with the buttonholes on the opposite side. Sew each button to the cardigan.

Binding off in Rib Stitch

When you see the directions "BO in rib" you have a few choices. There are several BOs that look great in rib:

1. Knit/Purl BO: Simply knit the knit sts and purl the purl sts as you work a normal BO. This looks better than a regular all-knitted BO because the alternating sts keep the edge from flaring out, but you can still see a little chain that lies across the top. The chain gives it a nice meaty dimensional edge that, in my opinion, looks nice at the bottom of a garment but not as nice on a front edge.

2. Tubular BO: This technique makes a very pretty and stretchy edge, but it takes extra time and concentration. This is a great technique to use on the bound-off edge of a collar or a front button band. The edge is completely invisible and appears to roll from the front to the back side, almost looking like a folded hem (see Techniques for instructions).

3. Grafted or Kitchener St BO: This lesser-known BO technique is identical in appearance to the Tubular BO, but it's worked a little differently. I find this technique easier to follow than the tubular BO, but it requires a little extra setup. The sts are distributed over 2 needles, with all the purl sts on 1 needle, and all the knit sts on another, then you use the Kitchener st (see Techniques) to graft the two sets of sts together. I like this technique because I already know how to do the Kitchener st, so it seems very natural to me.

Here's how to set it up:

a. Beg with your sts on a circular needle. Shift the sts to the other end of the needle (opposite from the side with the working yarn).

b. Take another circular needle, preferably 1 size smaller than the needle that you made the ribbing with, and fold the needle in half so both tips are held parallel in your right hand. Arrange the 2 needles so 1 is in front and the other is in back. Hold the needle with the ribbing in your left hand.

c. Beg transferring sts to the smaller needles: Slip the knit sts to the front needle and the purl sts to the back needle (slip all sts purlwise). When you get to the end of the row, turn the work—you'll be set up to beg your BO with the working yarn in the right position.

d. Beg binding off using the Kitchener st: Cut the yarn about 3 times longer than the width of the piece you're binding off and thread end onto a yarn needle (YN). Insert the YN into the front st as if to purl, and pull the yarn through. Insert the YN into the back st as if to knit, and pull the yarn through. *Insert the YN into the front st as if to knit, pull the st off the needle, then insert the YN into the next st on the front needle as if to purl, pull the yarn through both sts. Insert the YN into the back st as if to purl, pull the st off the needle, then insert the YN into the next st on the back needle as if to knit, pull the yarn through both sts. Rep from the * to the last 2 sts. Insert the YN into the front st as if to knit, pull the st off the needle, then insert the YN into the back st as if to knit, pull the st off the needle and pull the yarn through both sts.

Attach Pockets

Position pockets on the fronts of the cardigan just above the lower ribbing of the sweater, and about 2" (5 cm) away from the button band. Using mattress st and matching yarn, sew the pockets to the sweater as neatly as possible. Using a sewing needle and thread, sew a button to the sweater on inside of each pocket, aligning it with the buttonhole.

Plackets on Cuffs

Lap the button placket over the opposite side of the cuff. Using small neat sts, sew the CO edge of the placket down. Position buttons on the cuff aligning them with the buttonholes in the placket. Sew down each button using a sewing needle and thread.

Weave in ends. Block again if desired.

jalopy belt

THIS REVERSIBLE BELT FEATURES a chevron stripe pattern and a braided tie for closure. Show off the stripe pattern by wrapping the belt backward with the bow in the back like an obi belt. Worn in any orientation, it looks great over a long tunic to add a little waist definition, or through the belt loops of your favorite jeans. This is a great project to keep in your purse because of its small size, and the pattern is easy to memorize.

FINISHED SIZE

About 1½" (3.8 cm) wide and 28" (71 cm) long; ties 18" (45.5 cm) long.

YARN

Sport (#2 Fine)

Shown here: Blue Sky Alpacas Alpaca Silk (50% baby alpaca, 50% silk; 146 yd [133 m]/50 g). #126 Brick (A) and #137 Sapphire (B), 1 skein each.

NEEDLES

Size U.S. 2 (2.75 mm): set of 3 double-pointed (dpn).

Adjust needle size if necessary to obtain the correct gauge.

NOTIONS

Stitch marker

Yarn needle

GAUGE

15 sts = 1½" (3.8 cm) and 31 rnds = 4" (10 cm) in Chevron Patt.

Stitch Guide

**Stripe Pattern
(any number of sts):**

RNDS 1 AND 2: Color B.

RNDS 3 AND 4: Color A.

RNDS 5–12: Rep Rnds 1–4 five times.

RNDS 13–16: Color B.

RNDS 17–20: Color A.

RNDS 21–60: Rep Rnds 13–20 five times.

Rep Rnds 1–60 for patt.

**Chevron Pattern
(over 30 sts):**

RND 1: [Ssk, k5, M1, k1, M1, k5, k2tog] twice.

RND 2: Knit.

Rep Rnds 1 and 2 for patt.

When working with so few stitches on double-pointed needles, I find it much easier to distribute my stitches over just 2 needles: the front half of the stitches on one needle and the back half of the stitches on another needle. Give it a try; I'm sure you'll be surprised how fast your knitting goes!

Notes

Belt is worked in the rnd on small dpn to produce a dense fabric. The main part of the belt is knit first. Then long strands of yarn are attached to each end that are braided into cords and tied into a bow for closure.

As you work each stripe of color, carry the unused color along the inside of the belt by twisting it together with the used color once before you begin the first stitch of each row. This will minimize the number of loose ends to weave in at the end.

Make-One Increase (M1): For the best-looking result when working this increase (see Techniques), make a backward loop on your right thumb and transfer it to your right needle as if to cast on a stitch.

Chevron Base

With color A, CO 10 sts. Divide sts evenly over 2 dpn. Pm and join to work in the rnd, being careful not to twist sts.

RND 1: Knit.

RND 2: [K2, M1, k1, M1, k2] twice—14 sts.

RND 3: Switch to color B, knit.

RND 4: [K3, M1, k1, M1, k3] twice—18 sts.

RND 5: Knit.

RND 6: [K4, M1, k1, M1, k4] twice—22 sts.

RND 7: Switch to color A, knit.

RND 8: [K5, M1, k1, M1, k5] twice—26 sts.

RND 9: Knit.

RND 10: [K6, M1, k1, M1, k6] twice—30 sts.

Main Part of Belt

Beg Stripe Patt and work as foll:

Knit 1 rnd.

Work in Chevron Patt until piece meas 28" (71 cm) from CO, or until it almost wraps around your natural waist. Remember that the belt will stretch with wear, so make it at least 2" (5 cm) shorter than desired. With sts distributed evenly over 2 dpn, join them using the Kitchener st (see Techniques).

Finishing
Braids

STEP 1: Cut 4 lengths of color A about 48" (122 cm) long.

STEP 2: Thread the yarn needle with the 4 strands held together, leaving a short tail.

STEP 3: Insert the needle into the tip of the belt in the center about ¼" (6 mm) from the edge, and pull through just until the short tail goes through the hole.

STEP 4: Remove the needle from the strands, and adjust the length of the strands so all the ends align— there should be 8 strands about 24" (61 cm) long dangling from the belt.

Rep steps 1–4, but use color B instead of A, and insert the needle just to the right of the first set of strands. Then rep steps 1–4 once more using B again, but insert the needle just to the left of the first set of strands.

Neatly braid the three groups of strands all the way to the tips. Tie an overhand knot in the end leaving about 1" (2.5 cm) of loose strands to form a tassel. Trim to make the ends neat, if necessary.

Rep at the other end of the belt.

Blocking

Wet-block the belt if desired. Lay the belt on an ironing board, and layer a smooth dishcloth over it. With the steam setting on your iron turned on, press the belt flat. Flip the belt over, and rep on the other side.

abbreviations

beg(s)	begin(s); beginning		**rem**	remain(s); remaining
BO	bind off		**rep**	repeat(s); repeating
cir	circular		**Rev St st**	reverse stockinette stitch
cm	centimeter(s)		**rnd(s)**	round(s)
cn	cable needle		**RS**	right side
CO	cast on		**sl**	slip
cont	continue(s); continuing		**S2kp**	Sl 2, K1, psso (double decrease)
dec(s)('d)	decrease(s); decreasing; decreased		**Sk2p**	Sl 1, K2tog, psso (double decrease)
dpn	double-pointed needles		**sl st**	slip st (slip stitch purlwise unless otherwise indicated)
foll(s)	follow(s); following			
g	gram(s)		**ssk**	slip, slip, knit (decrease)
inc(s)('d)	increase(s); increasing; increase(d)		**st(s)**	stitch(es)
			ssp	slip, slip, purl (decrease)
k	knit		**St st**	stockinette stitch
kfb	knit into the front and back of same stitch		**tbl**	through back loop
			tog	together
k2tog	knit 2 stitches together		**w&t**	wrap and turn
k3tog	knit 3 stitches together		**WS**	wrong side
kwise	knitwise, as if to knit		**wyb**	with yarn in back
m	marker(s)		**wyf**	with yarn in front
mm	millimeter(s)		**yd**	yard(s)
M1	make one (increase)		**yo**	yarnover
oz	ounce		*****	repeat starting point
p	purl		******	repeat all instructions between asterisks
pfb	purl into front and back of same stitch			
			( )	alternate measurements and/or instructions
p2tog	purl 2 stitches together			
patt(s)	pattern(s)		**[ ]**	work instructions as a group a specified number of times
pm	place marker			
psso	pass slipped stitch over			
pwise	purlwise; as if to purl			

techniques

Cast-ons

Backward-Loop Cast-On

*Loop working yarn and place it on needle backward so that it doesn't unwind. Repeat from *.

Invisible Provisional Cast-On

Make a loose slipknot of working yarn and place it on the right needle. Hold a length of contrasting waste yarn next to the slipknot (or tie it together with the slipknot) and around your left thumb; hold working yarn over your left index finger. *Bring the right needle forward under waste yarn, over working yarn, grab a loop of working yarn (**Figure 1**), then bring the needle back behind the working yarn and grab a second loop (**Figure 2**). Repeat from * for the desired number of stitches. When you're ready to work in the opposite direction, place the exposed loops onto a knitting needle as you pull out the waste yarn.

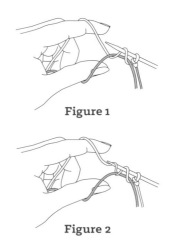

Figure 1

Figure 2

Bind-offs

Standard Bind-Off

Knit the first stitch, *knit the next stitch (two stitches on right needle), insert left needle tip into first stitch on right needle (**Figure 1**) and lift this stitch up and over the second stitch (**Figure 2**) and off the needle (**Figure 3**). Repeat from * for the desired number of stitches.

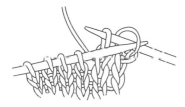

Figure 1

Figure 2

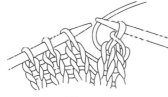

Figure 3

Tubular K1, P1 Rib Bind-Off

Also called the invisible ribbed bind-off, this method produces an extremely elastic edge that follows a knit-one, purl-one rib. The edge has a rounded appearance that when viewed straight down from above looks as though the stitches are continuous from the right side to the wrong side of the piece.

Cut the yarn, leaving a tail three times the width of the knitting to be bound off, and thread the tail onto a tapestry needle.

STEP 1: Working from right to left, insert the tapestry needle purlwise (from right to left) through the first (knit) stitch (**Figure 1**) and pull the yarn through.

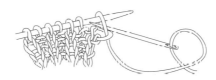

Figure 1

STEP 2: Bring the tapestry needle behind the knit stitch, then insert it knitwise (from left to right) into the second stitch (this will be a purl stitch; **Figure 2**), and pull the yarn through.

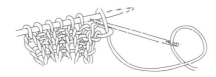

Figure 2

STEP 3: *Insert the tapestry needle into the first (knit) stitch knitwise and slip this stitch off the knitting needle (i.e., knit into the first st and slip it off the needle).

STEP 4: Bring the tapestry needle in front of the first (purl) stitch, then insert it purlwise into the second stitch (this will be a knit stitch; **Figure 3**), and pull the yarn through (i.e., purl into the second st and leave it on the needle).

Figure 3

STEP 5: Insert the tapestry needle into the first (purl) stitch purlwise and slip this stitch off the knitting needle (i.e., purl into the first st and slip it off the needle).

STEP 6: Bring the tapestry needle behind the knit stitch, then insert it knitwise into the second stitch (this will be a purl stitch; **Figure 4**), and pull the yarn through (i.e., knit into the second st and leave it on the needle).

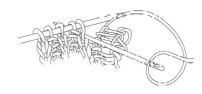

Figure 4

Repeat from * until one stitch remains on the knitting needle. If working in the round, end by inserting the tapestry needle purlwise through the first (knit) stitch of the round (the first one slipped off the needle) and draw the yarn through, then purlwise through the last stitch, and draw the yarn through.

Short-Rows
Knit Side

Work to turning point, slip next stitch purlwise (**Figure 1**), bring the yarn to the front, then slip the same stitch back to the left needle (**Figure 2**), turn the work around and bring the yarn in position for the next stitch—one stitch has been wrapped, and the yarn is correctly positioned to work the next stitch. When you come to a wrapped stitch on a subsequent row, hide the wrap by working it together with the wrapped stitch as follows: Insert right needle tip under the wrap (from the front if wrapped stitch is a knit stitch; from the back if wrapped stitch is a purl stitch; **Figure 3**), then into the stitch on the needle, and work the stitch and its wrap together as a single stitch.

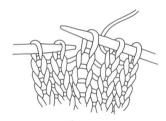

Figure 1

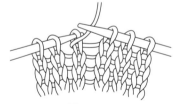

Figure 2

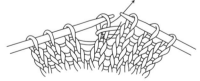

Figure 3

Purl Side

Work to the turning point, slip the next stitch purlwise to the right needle, bring the yarn to the back of the work (**Figure 1**), return the slipped stitch to the left needle, bring the yarn to the front between the needles (**Figure 2**), and turn the work so that the knit side is facing—one stitch has been wrapped, and the yarn is correctly positioned to knit the next stitch. To hide the wrap on a subsequent purl row, work to the wrapped stitch, use the tip of the right needle to pick up the wrap from the back, place it on the left needle (**Figure 3**), then purl it together with the wrapped stitch.

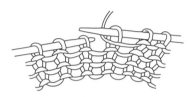

Figure 1

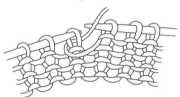

Figure 2

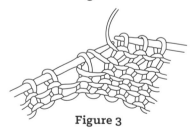

Figure 3

Seaming
Working Mattress Stitch in a Vertical Seam

STEP 1: Begin at the lower edge. The seam is worked between the first and second stitch of the row on both pieces. Insert the threaded needle into the right corner from the underside, and pull the yarn through (leave a 6" [15 cm] tail if the yarn is not already connected to your knitted fabric).

STEP 2: Next, insert the needle into the lower corner of the left piece from the topside. While the tip of the needle is still in the fabric, turn your needle so that it is vertical aligning it with the seam, and catch the bar that runs between the first and second stitch in the row. Pull the needle through.

STEP 3: Insert the needle in the topside of the opposite piece into the same hole that the yarn came from in the last step, turn your needle vertical, then run the needle under two bars, and pull the yarn through.

VERTICAL SEAM

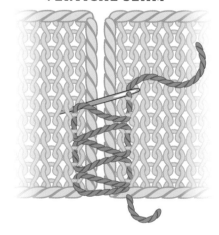

STEP 4: Repeat step 3 until the seam is done, adjusting the tension of your yarn to match the knitted stitches in the fabric.

> *Tip: I will sometimes pull the thread quite tight in a seam that requires extra structure, like a shoulder seam, or across the back of the neck.*

If your seam becomes misaligned, don't panic! It is perfectly fine to scoop up just one bar sometimes to even things out. When you do this be careful to keep the tension of the yarn even, so the fabric doesn't pucker.

> *Tip: You can reduce bulky seams by working closer to the edge, but beware, this can look sloppy if your tension isn't perfect. If your yarn is strong, you can pull the thread tight to hide the little holes that might form when working this way.*

Working the Mattress Stitch in a Horizontal Seam

This is worked in much the same way as the vertical seam, except instead of catching horizontal bars

HORIZONTAL SEAM

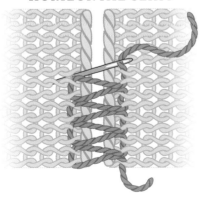

with the tip of your needle, you will catch the vertical legs of each stitch you're seaming.

Working the Mattress Stitch in a Diagonal, Curved, or Combination Seam

Sometimes you will need to attach a cast-on edge to a vertical selvage, or 2 diagonal edges, or a curved piece to a straight piece. Once you have mastered the vertical and horizontal mattress stitch, you can seam pretty much anything using the mattress stitch. The concept is the same: Catch about 2 strands of yarn on each side, always sticking your needle into the hole your yarn came from before. If you are sewing a combination seam, you should be aware that differences in row and stitch gauges will make things more complicated. You will need to adjust how many strands you catch on each side as you go.

COMBINATION SEAM

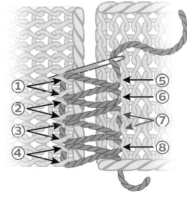

① 2 strands	⑤ 1 strand
② 2 strands	⑥ 1 strand
③ 2 strands	⑦ 2 strands
④ 2 strands	⑧ 1 strand

Grafting
Kitchener Stitch

Arrange stitches on two needles so that there is the same number of stitches on each needle. Hold the needles parallel to each other with wrong sides of the knitting together. Allowing about ½" (1.3 cm) per stitch to be grafted, thread matching yarn on a tapestry needle. Work from right to left as follows:

STEP 1: Bring tapestry needle through the first stitch on the front needle as if to purl and leave the stitch on the needle **(Figure 1)**.

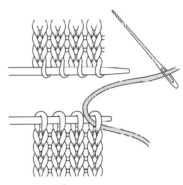

Figure 1

STEP 2: Bring tapestry needle through the first stitch on the back needle as if to knit and leave that stitch on the needle **(Figure 2)**.

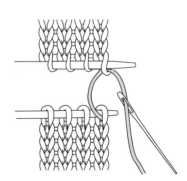

Figure 2

STEP 3: Bring tapestry needle through the first front stitch as if to knit and slip this stitch off the needle, then bring tapestry needle through the next front stitch as if to purl and leave this stitch on the needle (**Figure 3**).

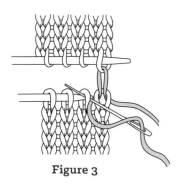

Figure 3

STEP 4: Bring tapestry needle through the first back stitch as if to purl and slip this stitch off the needle, then bring tapestry needle through the next back stitch as if to knit and leave this stitch on the needle (**Figure 4**).

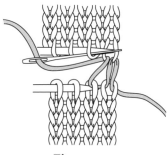

Figure 4

Repeat Steps 3 and 4 until one stitch remains on each needle, adjusting the tension to match the rest of the knitting as you go. To finish, bring tapestry needle through the front stitch as if to knit and slip this stitch off the needle, then bring tapestry needle through the back stitch as if to purl and slip this stitch off the needle.

Increases

Raised Make-One Increase (M1)

This type of increase is characterized by the tiny twisted stitch that forms at the base of the increase. Like the lifted method, it can slant to the right or the left, and you can separate the increases by the desired number of stitches to form a prominent ridge.

For circular yoke shaping, or when no slant is specified, use the slant of your choice.

Right Slant (M1R): Use the left needle tip to lift the strand between the needle tips from back to front (**Figure 1**), then knit the lifted loop through the front to twist it (**Figure 2**).

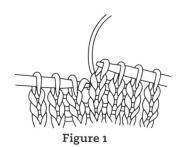

Figure 1

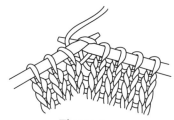

Figure 2

Left Slant (M1L): Use the left needle tip to lift the strand between the needle tips from front to back (**Figure 1**), then knit the lifted loop through the back to twist it (**Figure 2**).

Figure 1

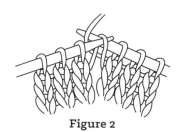

Figure 2

You can work these increases purlwise (M1P) by purling the lifted strand instead of knitting it.

Bar Increase
Knitwise (kfb)

Knit into a stitch but leave the stitch on the left needle (**Figure 1**), then knit through the back loop of the same stitch (**Figure 2**) and slip the original stitch off the needle (**Figure 3**).

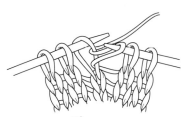

Figure 1

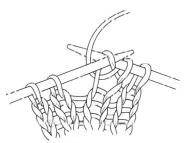

Figure 2

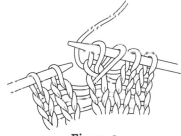

Figure 3

Purlwise (pfb)

Work as for a knitwise bar increase, but purl into the front and back of the same stitch.

Decreases
Slip, Slip, Knit (ssk)

Slip two stitches individually knitwise (**Figure 1**), insert left needle tip into the front of these two slipped stitches, and use the right needle to knit them together through their back loops (**Figure 2**).

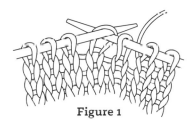

Figure 1

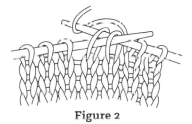

Figure 2

Slip, Slip, Purl (ssp)

This type of decrease slants to the left. Holding yarn in front, slip two stitches individually knitwise (**Figure 1**), then slip these two stitches back onto left needle (they will be twisted on the needle) and purl them together through their back loops (**Figure 2**).

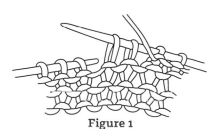

Figure 1

Figure 2

sources for yarn

Austermann
Distributed by Skacel
(800) 255-1278
skacelknitting.com

Berroco
1 Tupperware Dr., Ste. 4
North Smithfield, RI 02896
(401) 769-1212
berroco.com

Blue Sky Alpacas
PO Box 88
Cedar, MN 55011
blueskyalpacas.com

Cascade Yarns
PO Box 58168
1224 Andover Pk. E.
Tukwila, WA 98188
cascadeyarns.com

The Fibre Company
Distributed by Kelbourne Woolens
2000 Manor Rd.
Conshohocken, PA 19428
kelbournewoolens.com

Louet North America/ Gems
3425 Hands Rd.
Prescott, ON
Canada KOE ITO
louet.com

Madelinetosh
7515 Benbrook Pkwy.
Benbrook, TX 76126
madelinetosh.com

Malabrigo
(786) 866-6187
malabrigoyarn.com

Quince & Co.
quinceandco.com

Rowan
Green Lane Mill
Holmfirth, West Yorkshire
England HD9 2DX
+44 (0)1484 681881
knitrowan.com

USA: Westminster Fibers
165 Ledge St.
Nashua, NH 03060
(800) 445-9276
westminsterfibers.com

index

Add these new Interweave resources
offering stylish projects
to your knitting library

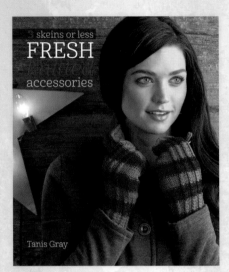

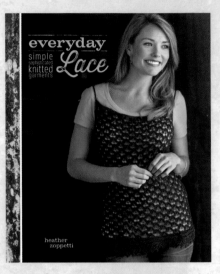

Brioche Chic
22 Fresh Knits for Women & Men
Mercedes Tarasovich-Clark
ISBN 978-1-62033-442-3
$26.99

3 Skeins or Less:
Fresh Knitted Accessories
Tanis Gray
ISBN 978-1-62033-673-1
$24.99

Everyday Lace
Simple, Sophisticated
Knitted Garments
Heather Zoppetti
ISBN 978-1-62033-134-7
$24.99

Available at your favorite retailer or

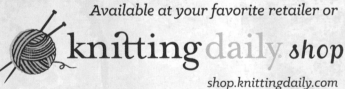

shop.knittingdaily.com

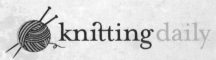

Join Knittingdaily.com, an online community that shares your passion for knitting. You'll get a free e-newsletter, free patterns, a projects store, a daily blog, event updates, galleries, knitting tips and techniques, and more. Sign up for *Knitting Daily* at **Knittingdaily.com.**

From cover to cover, *Interweave Knits* magazine presents great projects for the beginner to the advanced knitter. Every issue is packed full of smart, captivating designs, step-by-step instructions, easy-to-understand illustrations, plus well-written, lively articles sure to inspire. **Interweaveknits.com**